Between Therapist and Client

Editors:

Richard C. Atkinson
Gardner Lindzey
Richard F. Thompson

Between Therapist and Client
The New Relationship

REVISED EDITION

Michael Kahn

W. H. Freeman and Company

New York

Cover/text designer: Diana Blume

Library of Congress Cataloging-in-Publication Data

Kahn, Michael, 1924-
  Between therapist and client : the new relationship /
Michael Kahn. — Rev. ed.
  p. cm.
  Includes bibliographical references and index.
  ISBN 0-7167-3073-1 (pbk.)
  1. Psychotherapist and patient. 2. Psychotherapy. I. Title.
  RC480.8.K32 1996
  616.89'14—dc21   96-47559
                                                                  CIP

Printed in the United States of America

Third printing, 1999

For Jonathan

Contents

〜

Preface

In a J. D. Salinger story, the young author, Buddy Glass, receives this advice from his older brother:

> Remember before ever you sit down to write that you've been a reader long before you were ever a writer. You simply fix that fact in your mind, then sit very still and ask yourself, as a reader, what piece of writing in all the world Buddy Glass would most want to read if he had his heart's choice. The next step is . . . you just sit down shamelessly and write the thing yourself.[1]

I've been a client long before I ever was a therapist. This book is about the way I would like a therapist to be with me if I had my heart's choice.

The subtitle, *The New Relationship*, has, as I hope will become clear, two meanings. First, it means that in the field of psychotherapy, the beginnings of reconciliation between previously competing traditions open new possibilities for the way therapists relate to clients. Second, it means that in successful therapy the therapist provides for the client a relationship unlike any the client has had before.

For some time it has seemed to me that the training of psychotherapists would be helped by a book that brought together two major therapeutic traditions that have been separated through a series of sociological accidents. The two traditions are the humanistic psychologist's concern for a warm and empathic clinical relationship and the psychoanalyst's interest in bringing to the surface the unconscious aspects of that relationship—that is, the phenomena of transference and countertransference.

For several years I have been teaching a course that explores the possibilities of that integration; this book is the outgrowth of that course. I hope that it will prove useful to student therapists trying to keep their bearings on what can be turbulent and very confusing seas. I hope it may also be useful to practicing therapists who may not have had time to keep up with some of the most interesting recent developments in contemporary thinking about the clinical relationship. And though the book is addressed to therapists, it would give me pleasure if people who are not practicing clinicians found it interesting. I have tried to make it accessible to them, as well as to therapists.

The book contains many brief clinical illustrations. In most instances, I have indicated whether they are taken from my own practice or are borrowed from other authors. When neither of those attributions appear, the illustration has been invented, although probably none of them is truly invented. It's just that I no longer remember which clients taught them to me.

Many people have helped me in the course of writing this book. My (very) significant other, Virginia Kahn, and my colleagues Jeff Shapiro and Brant Cortright read the entire manuscript chapter by chapter, and, in addition to making invaluable suggestions, gave me support and encouragement. Diane Cimino Maass, my project editor [on the original and the revised edition], lovingly saw this book through from manuscript to completion, proofread it, and saw to its visual aesthetics. My sister Maggie

Tuteur, and my colleagues Karen Peoples, Bill Littlewood, Dean Elias, and Jacqueline West gave me significant assistance on one or more chapters. Donald P. Spence and Dale G. Larson read an early version of the manuscript and made valuable suggestions. Harvey Peskin graciously helped me purge the book of the most glaring of my prejudices. My brother, John Tuteur, an English scholar, generously gave me stylistic help. My friend and colleague Jack Clareman has supported me through the writing of this book in more ways than I can name. And like most teachers and therapists, I am aware that much of what I know I have learned from my students and my clients. My thanks to all.

Michael Kahn
August 1990

Notes on the revised edition

Since the first edition was completed, it has become increasingly clear how influential Merton Gill and Heinz Kohut have become. Gill has died and his intellectual descendants have attracted a great deal of interest as they have carried his work forward, exploring the concept variously called *social constructivism* (Irwin Hoffman) and *intersubjectivity* (Robert Stolorow). That seems to me an important concept, and I have added a consideration of it to this edition. Kohut's star continues to rise in the psychotherapeutic firmament; his self psychology has become more and more prominent and its influence is widely felt. It seems more important than ever that a therapist be aware of his contribution. For this edition, I have tried to clarify the nature of that contribution, and I've added a bit more to my original discussion of his work.

In this edition I have given more space to the concept of *projective identification,* and I have also acknowledged the importance of feminist consciousness to the broadening and deepening of relational psychotherapy, which is a generic term for what is explored in this book. Finally, I have added a discussion of how changes in health-care economics are affecting relational therapy.

I am grateful to Thomas A. Bergandi, Penina Frankel, Lynn Gillikin, F. Mel Madden, and Maria Cecilia Zea, who reviewed the first edition to give me advice for this one. My editor, Jonathan Cobb, has seen this book through two editions. He has been much more than an editor. He has been a gentle writing teacher and a good friend. I cannot imagine having completed either edition without him. Thus it is to him this book is gratefully dedicated.

Michael Kahn
October 1996

Between Therapist and Client

① Why Study the Relationship?

~

When I was a graduate student, I once asked a teacher of mine, a therapist of many years' experience, if he got bored doing clinical work. He thought it over and then replied that he'd been bored infrequently. "The more I've learned about the relationship, the more interesting the work has become," he said.

"The *relationship*?" I asked.

"I think so," he said. "It seems there are long periods when nothing very new is revealed about the client's symptoms or history. But that certainly isn't true about the relationship. I think I learn more about that every year, and the more I learn, the more it keeps me on my toes. There is so much going on every minute, I can't possibly stay with it all, and sometimes it goes so fast that I'm busy figuring out what I want to do about it. All of that seems so interesting, it would be hard to get bored."

"But why so much attention to the relationship?" I asked.

He looked puzzled for a moment. "Because the relationship *is* the therapy," he said.

Now I was puzzled. I was at the time deeply immersed in learning about analytic insights and how they are discovered and revealed to the client. I thought *that* was the therapy, and I told him so.

"Insight is important," he said. "But it's certainly not enough. I think the future lies in understanding the nature of the relationship between the therapist and the client."

That was more than thirty years ago, and I have come to believe that he was ahead of his time. I think he was right when he said that the therapist–client relationship itself holds enormous therapeutic potential, and I have discovered that he was also right when he said that attending to that relationship can be immensely interesting.

In this book I will suggest some ways to look at the clinical relationship and some actions the therapist can take to help the client as the relationship develops. I'm going to look at how some of the important thinkers in our field have variously conceptualized the relationship and how they have advised us to deal with it. Then I will offer a synthesis of those views to provide the therapist with some useful guidelines for working with clients.

There are two main reasons for making a careful study of the clinical relationship. First, it is risky not to. Much that goes on between therapist and client is subtle indeed. And subtle or not, each small vagary is likely to be charged with extreme importance for the client. The therapy and even the client can be damaged when the therapist is insufficiently aware of how easy it is to get into trouble.

Most beginning clinicians understand that it is important to live by the basic ground rules of therapy. Confidentiality must be observed, and the boundaries of the therapeutic relationship must be respected: we must remember every moment that our clients are neither friends nor lovers. Most therapists know these rules, but until one has grasped just how subtle and complex the relationship can be and how important the therapist becomes to the client, one is likely to underestimate how easy it is to damage the therapy. The slightest breach of confidentiality can be magnified by the client into a major betrayal; a chance encounter with a client outside the consulting room can evolve into a problematic social situation and have serious repercussions. An offhand remark or thoughtless joke can cause pain or confusion the client may not be able to acknowledge. None of these is likely to cause irreparable harm, but a sophisticated alertness to the vagaries of the relationship will minimize the chances of such slips, and, should they occur, will put the therapist in a stronger position to rectify the oversights and even make productive use of them.

The second reason for attending to the relationship is that it gives one a major therapeutic advantage. Awareness of the subtleties and changes in the relationship provides the therapist with a powerful tool, perhaps the most powerful therapeutic tool of all. I will try to show why that is true and how that tool may be used in our work with clients.

In psychodynamic therapy, which includes the various psychoanalytic-based therapies (among them, of course, self psychology), object relations therapies, Gestalt therapies, and various body-oriented therapies, awareness of the relationship is an indispensable tool. And even practitioners who choose not to deal explicitly with the relationship, such as behavior therapists, cognitive therapists, and advice-giving counselors, will avoid a good many pitfalls if they are sophisticated about what can happen in the relationship between therapist and client.

Five Propositions

This, then, is a book about understanding and dealing with the clinical relationship. It is built around the following propositions.

1. Insight is not enough. Even many years after the early clinicians discovered this, I suppose most therapists still experience (at least occasionally) the frustration and disappointment of uncovering and conveying a really good insight, only to discover it doesn't prompt much change in the client. Insight is necessary—but not sufficient.

2. The ingredient that needs to be added to insight is an understanding of the nature of the relationship and the way the therapist deals with it. Practically all schools of therapy agree that this understanding is needed. When they do disagree, it is over the nature of that relationship and how the therapist should deal with it.

3. One of the reasons the therapist–client relationship has such therapeutic potential is that it is the one relationship in the client's life that is actually happening during the therapy hour. During that time all other relationships are more abstract, more distant.

4. There was a time when selecting a training program meant choosing between a program that taught you how to understand the relationship and one that encouraged you to develop an accepting warmth toward the client. It was hard to find one that did both. The programs that emphasized the relationship also encouraged the therapist to adopt a stance of cool, distant "neutrality," so as not to influence the developing relationship. Only those therapists studying in programs with a heavily psychoanalytic emphasis, then, were taught very much about either the subtle complexities

of the therapeutic relationship or the ways it might be handled for the benefit of the client.

5. In recent years, however, there has been a marked rapprochement between therapists who understand and work with the complexities of the relationship and those who understand the need for that relationship to be warm and humane. A student no longer has to choose between the two.

A Short History of the Relationship

A brief look at the way our profession has regarded the clinical relationship through the years will add perspective to our explorations. Then in the following chapters we'll look in more detail at the ideas of Sigmund Freud, Carl Rogers, Merton Gill, and Heinz Kohut, as we begin to construct a way of using the relationship in the practice of psychotherapy.

The Freudian beginnings

It is important to remember that psychotherapy began as a medical specialty. Physicians, particularly nineteenth-century physicians, were trained to believe that what mattered was what you did to and for the patient; the relationship itself, sometimes contemptuously dismissed as "bedside manner," was considered irrelevant. Sigmund Freud and his co-worker Josef Breuer[1] were physicians, with the attitudes and assumptions that implied. In their early work together, in the 1880s and 1890s, they were trying to cure the condition called hysteria by figuring out what to do—that is, how to treat the condition as you would treat any disease. In the next chapter, we will follow Freud's path from a no-nonsense medical stance to an ever-growing conviction that the relationship between analyst and patient is crucial,* that it is invariably intense, mysterious, and very complex, however it might appear on the surface. As we will see, this view of the clinical relationship included the remarkable observation that patients transfer to the therapist their attitudes, feelings, fears, and wishes from long ago. Freud came to believe it essential that the therapist recognize this transference and know how to respond to it. He believed it had the power to hinder or further the treatment, depending on how it was dealt with. Eventually he saw the transference as the therapist's central opportunity and the fulcrum of therapeutic leverage.

In the century that followed Freud's early work with transference, this line of thought underwent some dramatic developments. Freud's way of being with his patients was active and engaged. As he reports it in his published case studies,[2] his approach was very different from the picture we have today of the silent, detached analyst. Sometimes he talked as much as the patient, carrying on a real dialogue. If a patient was hungry, he might serve a snack. To support one of his patients, he took up an annual collection of money from his psychoanalytic colleagues. And so on.

The early analysts, following much of what Freud preached, if not what he practiced, believed that the best service they could render their patients was to get out of the way as much as possible. They sat out of sight, and much of the time they kept quiet. They had three reasons for this approach.

First, they believed, following Freud, that the patient's difficulty came primarily from internal psychic conflict:

---

*I prefer to speak of "clients" rather than "patients" because I see the people I work with not as sick but rather as people with problems like my own, trying to grow as I am trying to grow. I will use *patient* when I discuss Freud's beliefs, since his model was so markedly doctor–patient; elsewhere I will use *client*.

conflict between wish and fear, conflict between incompatible wishes. If, then, they managed to keep quiet and let patients find their way into the expression of their deepest wishes and fears, those conflicts would emerge from the unconscious into the light of day. Once made conscious, those deep impulses and anxieties would have less power to dominate the patient.

Second, they believed that the transference would develop most fully if the analyst were a "blank screen" onto which the transference phenomena could be projected. Being a blank screen meant staying quiet and staying out of the way as much as possible, thus furnishing minimal cues about the actuality of the analyst's person.

Third, they believed that for therapy to progress, the analytic process required "optimal frustration." Thus the analyst seldom responded directly to the patient. In fact, the ideal was never to respond directly. Questions were not answered, pleasantries were not returned, compliments were not acknowledged, and accusations were not countered. The rule was "The analyst gives the patient nothing but interpretations." Analysts readily acknowledged that this was a frustrating situation for the patient. Say, "Good morning" and get nothing back but silence. Ask a question about what that last interpretation meant, and hear only silence. Tell your analyst you're really angry, and get no response. The early analysts believed the frustration thus evoked in their patients was the energizer that stirred inner conflicts and caused them to emerge from the depths.

As analysts gained experience with this way of working, it became clear to the most sensitive of them that if they were going to practice this highly disciplined approach to therapy, they would have to do so in the context of a great deal of loving compassion. Otherwise the patient would perceive the relationship as sadistic dominance. It's not easy to communicate compassion when your rules allow you to give nothing but interpretation. It probably can be done, but it takes a person of unusually large heart and unusually well developed communication skills. Freud himself seldom attempted it. He permitted himself a good deal of active engagement with his patients, whether or not that clashed with his beliefs.

So, theoretically, there were two possible ways of being truly therapeutic: one could be considerably more engaged with one's patients than the rules permitted, or one could be an unusually warm and compassionate person with an unusual capacity to communicate that compassion. Actually, I believe, the analysts were caught in an impossible contradiction. On the one hand, they required themselves to maintain a relatively severe neutrality, and on the other hand, they needed to create a therapeutic ambiance of trust, security, and confidence.

What happened all too often was that the analyst became the deadpan, silence-at-all-costs modern psychoanalyst, ripe for parody. In her book *The Impossible Profession* Janet Malcolm relates the famous story of the patient who came to a session on crutches and swathed in bandages. The analyst, a consummate professional, said nothing, merely sat stonily and waited for the associations to begin.

It is crucial to note here that when psychoanalysts speak of being neutral, they do not mean being cold and inhuman. Neutrality implies keeping a respectful distance so that patients can find their own way, without having the analyst's ideas imposed upon them. It means respecting the patient's autonomy and integrity. It means allowing patients to set and to change the emotional tone of the relationship. It also means giving them confidence that you will offer consistency no matter what they do. That this honorable concept has led some analysts to act coldly toward their patients should in no way detract from its power and its usefulness. It remains a valuable concept.

Extreme nonresponsiveness has for some years been under increasing criticism from all sides. Many contemporary psychoanalysts find it countertherapeutic. And to most therapists trained outside the analytic institutes (and many inside) it seems ethically and humanly unacceptable.

At its worst, nonresponsiveness is seen by the client as hostility. Even at its best, unless the analyst is a truly remarkable human being, it's hard to imagine that the cause of human growth is served by such a cold and manifestly inhumane relationship. The early analysts have much to teach us about the clinical relationship (after all, they invented the subject), and we will do well to ponder their insights carefully. But fewer and fewer analysts themselves still cling to the cool, nonresponsive stance.

Carl Rogers and the humanistic revolution

The field of therapy was dominated by the psychoanalysts until the 1940s, when an American psychologist named Carl Rogers sounded a decidedly American response to this therapy of European origin.[3] As we will see in Chapter 3, his view of the clinical relationship was very different from that of the analysts, and it became hugely popular in the ensuing 30 years, particularly in the United States. Though there are probably fewer pure Rogerians practicing today than there were 20 years ago, Rogers' influence is still widespread and constitutes a major force in contemporary American thinking about psychotherapy.

The clinical relationship that Rogers proposed was radically different from the nonresponsiveness that had come to predominate in American psychoanalysis. He taught that the therapeutic attitude required empathy and "unconditional positive regard" for the client and genuineness on the part of the therapist. This stance led his followers to be far more responsive to their clients than the analysts were. Although the psychoanalytic influence remained strong in American clinics, the clients of an increasing number of psychologists and other counselors began to be treated in a much more human, and perhaps humane, fashion than many analysts' patients were.

The revolution of the 1960s

The 1960s had as profound an effect on psychotherapy as they did on all other aspects of American life. For one thing, Rogers' influence became significantly diluted by two forces of the decade. The first was the political climate. To the radical consciousness of the 1960s, the undemocratic psychoanalytic relationship was anathema, relying as it did on a severe power imbalance between therapist and client. Two of Rogers' main tenets, uncompromising respect for his clients and a firm refusal to impose interpretations upon them, made his approach less objectionable to this political consciousness. Nonetheless, even in Rogers' method the power imbalance remained: self-revelation was expected of clients, whereas therapists, however warm and respectful, rarely shared their own feelings. Therapists influenced by radical politics searched for ways to make the clinical relationship even more egalitarian than Rogers had done.

The second significant force of the 1960s was the encounter movement of the newly popular humanistic psychology.[4] This tradition emphasized authenticity and symmetry. Authenticity implied that the therapist should be as honest and as emotionally exposed as the client, and symmetry, echoing the politics of the day, demanded that the therapist be willing to do anything the client was asked to do. It's not clear whether Rogers understood genuineness to mean the same thing that the encounter psychologists meant by authenticity, but there is no doubt that in practice they were very different. Rogers and his students practiced genuineness in the context of gentleness and positive regard. The encounter people tended to view authenticity in a context of unrestrained confrontation; for them, what was therapeutic was the participation in an authentic relationship, *authentic* meaning that therapists would openly share whatever feelings their clients stirred in them. Hostility, boredom, excitement, sexual attraction, any feeling might be expressed; what mattered was the honest sharing.

Rogers was actively involved in the encounter movement and considered himself importantly influenced by it. Nonetheless, just as his concept of genuineness was practiced by others in a context very different from his own, his notion of positive regard was taken to extremes that he had almost certainly not intended: psychologists influenced by '60s viewpoints saw their mission as giving the client considerable, often physical, loving support, sometimes laced with confrontation. This influence can still be found, though in recent years it has usually been diluted by the increased conservatism of the culture.

The psychoanalysts respond

It could be expected that many psychoanalysts would be critical of these trends, and indeed they were. First, they were concerned that the new therapeutic style was extremely confusing to the client, who might well wonder whether the person sitting opposite was therapist, friend, or antagonist. And just whose needs was the therapist there to serve, anyway?

Second, they worried that, freed to follow any impulse, the therapist might act out the deepest countertransference feelings and thus severely exploit the client. *Countertransference,* a concept we will examine in detail in Chapter 6, was Freud's term for the unconscious feelings that the patient stirred in the analyst. The patient, Freud taught, can stimulate in the analyst a strong impulse to act out old dramas and to gratify old unsatisfied needs. The analyst was to protect the patient by unremitting vigilance against those impulses. "Authenticity" looked to the analysts like a license to carry and use dangerous weapons.

Third, they saw no way to understand and use the patient's transference if it were so hopelessly confounded by the freely expressed reality of their own personality.

It is interesting to note that in the 1990s that particular pendulum has begun to swing back, and the analysts themselves are starting to question their own conservative disapproval of countertransference disclosure. We will have occasion to examine this new trend in the chapters ahead.

Another force that flowered in the '60s continues to grow in importance: feminism. Feminism has taken many forms, some of them political and some more broadly cultural, and it is those cultural forms that concern us here. The writers we study in this book don't report being particularly influenced by the feminists; yet feminism has become such a pervasive cultural influence that it is hard to see how modern psychotherapeutic thought could have avoided being strongly shaped by it. A book that seems to typify the feminist point of view and to present it with uncommon clarity is Barbara Stevens Sullivan's *Psychotherapy Grounded in the Feminine Principle,* first published in

1989.[5] Her point of view is remarkably similar to that of the relational therapists described in this book. Indeed, Kohut is one of the authors she cites with approval. Her thesis is that the classic model of the detached therapist figuring out the problem for the patient is based on a masculine point of view and makes little room for the feminine. A more balanced therapy, she suggests, makes room for qualities of warmth and receptivity. Such a therapy acknowledges that the relationship *is* the therapy, that both therapist and client can view the therapy only through the lenses of their unconscious fantasies, and that both are affected and changed by what transpires. We will see that all of those characteristics are important aspects of the therapies of Gill and Kohut.

It is interesting to ponder what shifts in the cultural winds may have caused the relational therapies to flourish in the '90s and brought them to such prominence. It is not hard to believe that the increased respect accorded the feminine perspective is somehow involved.

Finally, the '60s trends in clinical practice caused a crucial issue to be joined: should the client be gratified or frustrated? The analysts held firmly that frustration is necessary to the therapeutic process. Their argument went like this: All humans are irresistibly drawn to gratification and can't be expected to choose hard work when gratification seems to be offered free (few people would dig ditches if they could get the same pay for doing nothing); in fact, however, the gratification offered in the therapist's office is illusory. It is built on the denial of great human truths: We are alone, we are mortal, we are imperfect, and the world around us is, if anything, even more imperfect. There are no free lunches and few affordable ones.

The analysts believe that to learn these lessons the childhood illusions of merger and bliss must be analyzed and laid to rest. Then people can accept the hard truths of self-reliance and seek real, if limited, gratifications, rather than illusions which will vanish as they walk out of the therapist's office. Gratifications offered by the therapist merely prolong the illusion that the ultimate gratifier is out there somewhere, waiting to be found.

I hardly need point out how radically different this view of reality is from the sunny optimism of Carl Rogers and the American humanists.

A period of controversy

Thus our field emerged from the '60s in a state of sharp controversy. Should we be warm or neutral? Should we lay back, or should we mix it up? Should we frustrate or gratify? Should we keep the boundaries of the relationship very strict, or should we chat with our clients, socialize with them, and make friends of them? And perhaps the most important controversy of all: Are we to discuss with clients their relationship with us? Is it important that they tell us their feelings about us? Is it important that we search for feelings about us that they're not telling? For some years it seemed that there were persuasive advocates at both extremes and not very many trying to thread their way down the center.

From an unexpected source: rapprochement

And then from within the psychoanalytic movement itself, from the very heart of the psychoanalytic establishment, a new set of voices began to be heard. Two of the most articulate and comprehensive of these voices were those of Heinz Kohut and Merton Gill.[6] Kohut argued persuasively that clients saw the cold, unyielding stance of some contemporary analysts as the most painful and destructive sort of rejection. This was just the sort of rejection by the client's family that had gotten him into trouble in the first place. Trying to cure it with more of the same was like pouring gasoline on the fire. Just as Rogers had talked of the central importance of empathy, Kohut, from inside the psychoanalytic movement—in fact, as a past president of the prestigious American Psychoanalytic Association—was now speaking of visible, demonstrated empathy as one of the most important qualities that therapists had to offer clients.

Meanwhile, Merton Gill, another therapist with impeccable psychoanalytic credentials, was pointing out the striking difference between the cool stance of some modern analysts and Freud's warm interactions with his patients. Gill reminded his colleagues that human civility was an important part of the analytic ambiance.

In spite of the similarities to Rogers' advocacy of warmth, neither Gill nor Kohut had become Rogerians. Rogers had placed no particular importance on encouraging the client to attend to and discuss the relationship with the therapist, nor had he given any weight to consideration of the unconscious. Gill and Kohut, on the other hand, were both psychoanalysts. Their therapies were built around the concept of the unconscious, and they held fast to the psychoanalytic notion that working with the relationship between therapist and client was of central importance. We will see in the chapters ahead how each of them interpreted that concept and how similar many of their ideas are. For now, it is enough to note that they have introduced a hugely important middle way between the schools of warm support and those of neutral transference analysis, a middle way that combines the advantages of warm engagement with the advantages of working actively with the relationship itself.

The sine qua non: nondefensiveness

These two psychoanalytic pioneers, as we will see, also added another major component to the kind of therapy they developed. Though they use different vocabularies, it is clear that each of them sees nondefensiveness as crucial. To Kohut, this attribute provides the essential context for the kind of interpretation and analysis necessary for successful therapy. But to Gill, nondefensiveness is what actually effects the therapy. Gill teaches that throughout our lives, beginning with our parents, we encounter people who have so much to defend that we learn, at worst, to keep our feelings to ourselves or, at best, to expect the expression of those feelings to be met with little more than a defensive riposte. This is not a criticism of the socializing community; it's just the way it is. The therapeutic relationship is crucially different in that expressed feelings about the therapist are met not with a defensive countermove but rather with warm encouragement to explore them further. This is a remarkable combining of the Freudian concern with the relationship and the Rogerian emphasis on warmth and support. Together with Kohut's insights, it opens a whole new path for the clinician.

It has probably occurred to you that nondefensiveness is a good deal easier to prescribe than to practice. When we are threatened in any way, the temptation to fight back, to explain, to justify, to one-up, to go coldly silent is almost overwhelming in all but saints, and there are few saints in our profession. Yet I hope you will find that once nondefensiveness is made an explicit goal and a manageable technique, once you have seen the enormous value it offers clients, you will find it increasingly possible to follow Kohut and Gill into this initially threatening, enormously fascinating, and extremely fruitful realm.

Existential psychology

One other therapeutic tradition deserves mention—existential psychology. Growing out of European existentialism, it flowered in America in the late 1950s and had a clear influence on the humanistic psychology of the 1960s. We will not examine it separately because its view of the clinical relationship is close to those of the authors we will study. But as a part of the humanistic psychology movement it has had a great impact and thus deserves a place in this historical survey.

Rollo May, perhaps the most articulate and influential of the American existential psychotherapists, once said that he hoped there would never be a school of existential psychotherapy, but rather that the insights of the existentialists would permeate all schools. He gives what is perhaps his central insight in "The Emergence of Existential Psychology":

> There is no such thing as truth or reality for a living human being except as he participates in it, is conscious of it, has some relationship to it. We can demonstrate at every moment of the day in our psychotherapeutic work that only the truth that comes alive, becomes more than an abstract ideal but is "felt on the pulse," only the truth that is genuinely experienced on all levels of being, . . . only this truth has the power to change a human being.[7]

An abstract discussion of the client's problems or history is not likely to produce much change. Existential therapy is sometimes called *Dasein* analysis. *Dasein* translates roughly as "being there." The idea, of course, is that therapy works when the client is really *there,* rather than merely talking about herself—a view that is shared by Rogers, Gill, and Kohut.

It should be noted that the authors we study in this book all saw their clients for long courses of therapy. Rogers sometimes saw clients for shorter periods than our other authors, but Freud, Gill, and Kohut often saw their clients for several years, and several sessions a week. The theories we will review in this book were developed in that context. Now we are entering a period in our profession when it seems likely that we will have fewer opportunities to practice long-term therapy. I trust such opportunities will not disappear entirely, but it does seem likely that the current approach to the economics of health care may require many therapists to include in their practice a significant amount of brief therapy.

Therapists with a psychodynamic orientation will almost certainly see this constraint as limiting the potential depth of their work. Nonetheless, it seems to me that the principles of the clinical relationship outlined in this book, the principles of Rogers, Gill, and Kohut, can still be usefully applied, even as we accept the limitations of brief therapy.

Some of the principles that will emerge in the pages ahead do indeed require a long relationship if they are to be fully realized. But for a client to be treated, even for a few sessions, in the way our authors recommend would almost certainly be healing to old wounds.

We will see that we are urged to be genuine, respectful, nondefensive, and affirming of the client's reality, and to let the client know we are doing our best to understand that reality. And, above all, we are urged to communicate to clients our empathy for their experience.

Whether the therapy is long or short, to be treated that way is remarkably powerful. We might also note that the phenomena of transference and countertransference occur instantly in any relationship, and thus even in brief therapy they will be available for exploration, however limited.

If the therapist is permitted only five or ten sessions, the treatment won't be the same as years of therapy. But it will be a lot better than nothing.

From Dilemma to Dialectic

The old dilemma that required the clinician to choose between empathic warmth and active exploration of the relationship are being transformed by modern workers into dialectic. Thus the possibility of a new synthesis arises. In the chapters that follow we will look at this transformation in detail and then explore the emerging synthesis, as well as the clinical style and technique it implies.

Though it may sound as if I think that all the dilemmas have now been resolved, I am not so naive. The great questions of psychotherapy will never be definitively answered. Nonetheless, some interesting congruences are beginning to appear in the field. In spite of continuing sharp controversies and differences even among sympathetic colleagues, there is a growing unity of thought about ways of dealing with these issues in therapy. And these congruences can provide a useful set of guidelines for a beginning therapist. Every therapist eventually puts together his or her own method, but one needs to start somewhere. This book will suggest a place to start.

2

The Discovery of Transference

SIGMUND FREUD

Not long ago, teaching the ideas of Sigmund Freud to graduate students was an exercise in diplomacy and public relations. Freud was definitely out, and it took some doing to get students even to consider that he might be worth reading. Feminists were understandably concerned about the nineteenth-century Germanic sexism in his writing. Humanistic psychologists found him gloomy and discouraging, in sharp contrast to the optimism they were trying to promulgate. They also objected to his view of human beings as merely the highest form of animal, fearing that he omitted the spiritual, transcendent nature of the human being. Radicals found him authoritarian and disapproved of the power imbalance between analyst and patient.

One consequence of these reactions was that the Freudian insights disappeared from much of the clinical training outside the psychoanalytic institutes. It was as though English departments had stopped teaching Shakespeare because of his anti-Semitism or mathematics departments had suppressed Einstein because of his part in the chain of discoveries leading to the atom bomb.

Now, among clinical graduate students, that attitude is rapidly changing. Some residual prejudice against Freud remains, but it has greatly lessened, and the field of clinical practice is in a position to study his work more objectively, taking from it what is useful. Some influential feminist sociologists and psychologists, such as Nancy Chodorow,[1] consider themselves Freudians and are attempting to integrate Freudian thought into the new political awareness. Many feminists are coming to believe that it is difficult to understand the causes and effects of sexism—or for that matter, to understand the human mind—without the illumination of Freud's theory of the unconscious.

As we will see in later chapters, the humanistic tradition is at last finding avenues of rapprochement with psychoanalysis. And as 1960s radicalism has softened, politically conscious psychologists have come to look for ways to make psychotherapy more egalitarian without discarding the valuable contributions of psychoanalysis.

All of these changes have reduced the antipathy to Freud and made it possible once again to incorporate his insights into the development of modern psychotherapy.

In the years since Freud's death, psychology has moved on, building on his and his colleagues' work, developing theories of clinical practice more sophisticated and more effective than the psychoanalysis he left us. Nonetheless, he is the most powerful, original, and influential writer psychology has produced; studying the mind without studying Freud is like studying evolution without Darwin.

It is not just the psychologist who is limited by ignoring Freudian theory; it is all of us. Freud cast a light deep into the hidden recesses of the mind, making visible a vast new world. Our view of ourselves and others is made infinitely richer (if sometimes more unsettling) by that illumination. For therapists, part of that richness is what we can now recognize in our relationships with clients. Freud taught us how to see the remarkable drama that unfolds in the consulting room.

Let's look at how that development came about.

Breuer and Bertha: The Discovery of Transference

At the very beginning of his career Freud witnessed a remarkable event. His friend and mentor, Josef Breuer, was treating an attractive young woman for hysteria. He saw this woman, whose name was Bertha, twice a day, often in her bedroom. He talked about her constantly. It was clear to Freud that Breuer was fascinated by Bertha. And it shortly became clear to him that the fascination was by no means one-way. Breuer was summoned to the house one evening to find Bertha in great distress. She announced to him that she was pregnant with his child. Breuer felt absolutely certain that she was a virgin. And, indeed, the "pregnancy" turned out to be entirely hysterical.

In Chapter 1 we noted that Freud, a nineteenth-century physician, had begun with a very mechanical view of the therapeutic relationship. Observing what had happened between Breuer and his patient, he began to understand that the therapeutic relationship was much deeper and more complex than anything seen in the conventional view of the doctor–patient relationship. For the rest of his life he struggled to understand the nature of the therapist–patient relationship and how it could best be dealt with. To increase his understanding, he looked to his most important source of information: his own and his colleagues' patients. As he scrutinized those relationships, he made two discoveries that will particularly concern us.

The Theory of Templates

In our earliest relationships we establish templates, patterns into which we tend to fit all of our subsequent relationships, or at least all of our *important* subsequent relationships.[2] If I had a warm and supportive relationship with my father, it is likely that I will tend to see male authority figures in a positive light. I will seek out that kind of relationship, will expect good things from it, and will behave in ways to maximize the chance that it will indeed turn out well. If, on the other hand, my father was particularly critical of me, it is likely that I will tend to see men in authority as critical and to relate to them in that way. If I had to struggle with my siblings for my parents' attention, it is probable that I will see my peers as competitors for scarce resources. And so on.

The spoken associations of Breuer's patient Bertha led Freud to believe that she had been particularly troubled by unresolved unconscious sexual feelings for her father and even an unconscious wish to bear his child. Freud considered it likely she would consequently have such feelings and wishes about Breuer. Early in her life she had established that way of relating to men in positions of authority. Further, he observed, she would tend to relate similarly to any man to whom she was attracted; that is, she would have sexual feelings and would also tend to repress them. Because such feelings were an unconscious replay of incestuous wishes, she would view them as forbidden. It is easy to imagine that her unconscious ambivalences would cause Bertha difficulty in her life. Indeed, the tendency to force our contemporary relationships into old patterns is likely to cause difficulty for all of us. But as we will see, it can be an invaluable guide to a therapist.

The Repetition Compulsion

The second discovery of Freud's that will help us in our exploration of the clinical relationship is the one he called the *repetition compulsion*. By this he meant that we have a need to create for ourselves repeated replays of situations and relationships that were particularly difficult or troubling in our early years. This was one of Freud's truly great discoveries. We have all met people who go to remarkable lengths to recreate situations that had bad endings.

Freud puts it like this:

> We have come across people all of whose human relationships have the same outcome: such as the benefactor who is abandoned in anger after a time by each of his *protégés*, however much they may otherwise differ from one another, and who thus seems doomed to taste all the bitterness of ingratitude; or the man whose friendships all end in betrayal by his friend; or the man who time after time in the course of his life raises someone else into a position of great private or public authority and then, after a certain interval, himself upsets that authority and replaces him by a new one; or, again, the lover each of whose love affairs passes through the same phases and reaches the same conclusion.[3]

The repetition compulsion is a phenomenon that causes dismay when we see it in our friends and despair when we see it in ourselves. And it is a phenomenon with which we are continually occupied in our work with clients. Like so much of human behavior, this seems paradoxical: Why go to such trouble to create a situation sure to cause one pain and frustration?

At first glance, it looks as though the person were trying over and over to put a happy ending on an earlier situation, one that was anything but happy. But as we will see, it doesn't work that way. Should a replay turn out happily, the experience seems spoiled, and it's back to the drawing board to recreate the old unhappy situation once again. Freud's view was that the very painfulness of the original situation was fixating, driving one repeatedly to behave as though one were unconsciously trying to understand what had happened and why it had happened. We might thus expect Bertha to go to considerable lengths to put herself in situations reminiscent of her relationship with her father. Few of us would be surprised to learn that Bertha's father had actually been seductive toward her and that she had found in Breuer a man who was more than willing to play his part in a drama of seductive teasing.

We have noted that though a person in the grip of the repetition compulsion seems to be seeking a happy ending, such an interpretation is misguided. The situation with a happy ending would no longer be the *original* situation, which is defined by conflict, frustration, and guilt. So if Bertha ever had found a loving, attractive, slightly older man who returned her love and of whom all her friends and family approved, she would have been strongly motivated to lose interest in him and to resume the search for a desirable but forbidden man.

Since the repetition compulsion operates everywhere, it is no surprise that it turns up in the client's relationship with the therapist. And as we will see in the chapters ahead, that situation presents the therapist with valuable opportunities. For one thing, it brings important parts of the client's life into the therapist's office, where they can be studied at close range. Further opportunities will become clear as we proceed.

Transference

According to Freud, when people enter therapy, the way they see and respond to the therapist and the reactions they set out to provoke are influenced by two tendencies: they will see the relationship in the light of their earliest ones, and they will try to engender replays of early difficult situations. To these perceptions, responses, and provocations Freud gave the name *transference,* meaning that the client transfers onto the therapist the old patterns and repetitions.[4]

As we will see in our discussion of Gill (Chapter 4), and particularly in the chapter on Kohut (Chapter 5), Freud's followers realized that transference could in some cases take a form other than the simple repetition of how the client had *experienced* the original relationship: it could also represent a replay of how the client had *wished* it were. So if I saw my father as aloof and disapproving, I might see my analyst that way too, or I might see him or her as warm and loving, thus giving myself the "father" I always wanted. And I might switch back and forth between these views.

The transference phenomenon is sufficiently strong to get itself expressed regardless of the gender of the therapist. While it is undoubtedly the case that at first a male therapist is more likely to draw a father transference and a female therapist a mother transference, eventually all the major relationships will get transferred onto the therapist, man or woman.

Two examples

One of my clients spent a good deal of the first year of her therapy raging at me. It didn't much matter what I did or didn't do; I was generally no good. Gradually she was able to tell me about being abandoned by her father at a very early age. It wasn't just that he had left her and her mother to fend for themselves; she had adored and completely trusted him. As I learned about this experience, I was able to accept her rage more easily and to understand why she needed to direct it toward me.

A male client often expressed concern about whether or not I liked him, admired him, preferred him to other clients. He had grown up in a cold home, with very constricted parents from a European culture that did not encourage the "coddling" of children. He was starved for validation. Kohut called this a "mirror transference," teaching that it represented the client's wish for affirmation never received.

Transference in everyday life

Freud has a featured place in the intellectual history of the twentieth century, not primarily because he pioneered a new approach to the treatment of emotional disturbance, but because he added significantly to our knowledge of ourselves. The theory of transference is a good example of his contribution. It doesn't apply only to clients and therapists; it applies to all of us in all our relationships. Everywhere we go, we are ceaselessly replaying some aspect or other of our early life. We can see it in our authority relations; we can see it in our love affairs; we can see it in our friendships; we can see it in our business dealings. Becoming sensitive to the phenomena of transference doesn't only make us better clinicians; it also gives us a new appreciation for the astonishing design of our relationships. That design might be thought of as poetic or, more accurately perhaps, as musical.

The composers of the eighteenth and nineteenth centuries used a form they called the sonata. (The opening movements of Mozart's and Beethoven's symphonies are examples.) In the sonata all the themes that are going to appear are stated at the beginning. From there on, everything that occurs in the form is a variation, development, or replay of those themes. The listener's understanding and appreciation of those themes is continually increased. The power of that design is one of the reasons music of that period is apparently going to be played forever. One might think of one's first relationships as the themes of one's interpersonal life and all subsequent relationships as the development and recapitulation of those themes. We will see in the chapters ahead that this musical comparison gives us a productive way to view our clients.

Freud's way of understanding transference and of working with it evolved throughout his career. Following that evolution will help us grasp the concept.

Freud's early view of transference

Originally Freud saw the transference as being helpful if it consisted of positive feelings. Liking and wanting to please your therapist were seen as necessary motivations for the difficult journey. The only time positive feelings were not helpful, he noted, was when they had a strong erotic component that became so demanding and intractable that they interrupted or even wrecked the therapy.

A case in point is Bertha's powerful erotic transference to Breuer. Had the craft of psychoanalysis been sufficiently advanced at the time, Breuer might have been able to interpret the transference in its early stages and thus to head off a sharp rupture of the therapy. The sad fact is that after the evening when Bertha told him she was pregnant, her treatment stopped, and they never saw each other again. But even if Breuer had seen what was coming and attempted to interpret it as transference, and even if his own countertransference—his own emotional involvement with his patient—had not been so strong, it's not certain he would have succeeded. Freud remarked that there are times when it is simply impossible to persuade a patient to give up the demand for the analyst's love and to accept the transference interpretation; then, according to Freud, the analysis is at an end.[5]

The patient's inevitable *negative* feelings toward the therapist he saw as intermittent obstacles. The therapist's task was to "interpret the transference": that is, to help the patient understand the true (i.e., childhood) origins of those feelings, freeing the therapy from the burden of, say, suspicion or anger.

In one of his earliest published cases, Freud writes of his patient Dora, who, to his surprise, abruptly terminated treatment.[6] Only on reflection did Freud realize he had missed the signs that a severe negative transference was brewing and that his failure to see and interpret it had been fatal to the analysis.

Early in his career, Freud thought it was important to help the patient see the ancient roots of his or her feelings only when the transference, whether erotic or negative, interfered with the patient's enthusiastic willingness to work with the therapist. Eventually he saw other reasons to focus the patient's attention on the transference; we'll look at those in a moment.

At first, then, Freud believed that interpreting transference was not the real work of psychoanalysis and should be undertaken only when the transference got in the way of that real work. The "real work" of analysis consisted of reconstructing ancient dramas from the patient's free associations. They had to be reconstructed because they had been repressed, and could not have been consciously recalled even if the patient wanted to remember them.

And since they had been repressed, they operated without the patient's awareness and control and therefore had terrible destructive power.

Freud thought of himself as an archaeologist of the mind. He saw his work as reconstructing the hidden, unconscious story of the patient's life from clues and fragments, as a physical archaeologist attempts to reconstruct a civilization by carefully exhuming and assembling fragments of artifacts and bits of architecture. Reconstructing the ancient dramas meant making conscious their previously unconscious aspects. When those aspects had been made conscious and "worked through" so that they could be "emotionally utilized" by the patient, they would no longer have the power to control the patient's life.

Working through and emotional utilization

Originally Freud had thought that merely discovering the unconscious dramas and explaining them to the patient would be sufficient for successful therapy. To his great disappointment, they were not. He discovered that "knowing" had many meanings. For example, patients could *know* intellectually that their guilt feelings were unjustified and *know* that their self-destructive patterns were generated by this guilt, and still, in an important sense, *not know* it. They could still hold the persistent old beliefs that predated the analysis. These beliefs might be partly conscious; in spite of the new knowledge, there might remain corners of consciousness in which the patients were not really *convinced* that they did not deserve their guilt, and were not really *convinced* that they brought punishment down on their heads in attempts to alleviate that guilt. Though these perceptions might be partly conscious, they were likely to be predominantly unconscious: "If we communicate our knowledge to him, he does not receive it; and that makes very little change in it."[7] That is, unconsciously the patient clings to the old beliefs and the old blindnesses, and thus real change is unlikely. "Working through" was the name Freud gave to the process whereby these insights could become so well integrated into the personality, both intellectually and emotionally, that the patient could give up the old neurotic patterns. Freud's term for this deepening process was "emotional utilization."[8] This was Freud's way of dealing with the theme with which we began this book: Insight is not enough.

How the insights were to be worked through and integrated into the patient's personality became the main challenge of psychoanalysis. The importance of this problem cannot be overstated. Most of the subsequent history of psychotherapy, down to our own day, and most of the history of the clinical relationship have consisted of attempts to solve it.

At first Freud thought that the way to permit the patient to work through insights was to have her encounter them over and over, in one context after another. That's why psychoanalysis took so long.

Early in my own psychoanalysis I learned how powerfully my life was influenced by guilt over fancied childhood sins. Then slowly, examining my life, I began to learn about the multitude of ways in which guilt manifested itself. I learned how it affected my work, how it shaped my relationships with women; I learned about its impact on my relations with my professors and with supermarket clerks. I came to think that when psychoanalysis succeeded, it did so by boring a symptom to death. My analyst was applying Freud's early view of how insight becomes worked through and produces change in the patient. That view is still a part of psychoanalytic theory. But Freud was to add to it something new and important.

Working through in the transference

A significant moment in the history of psychoanalysis arrived when two lines of Freud's thought met and merged: his concern with the problem of emotional utilization of insights and his study of the clinical relationship. He decided that the best place of all in which to work through the insights would be the relationship between the patient and the therapist: that is, the transference.[9]

This decision, as you can see, marked an important change in the way Freud saw the clinical relationship, and indeed it marked a major change in the way any therapist had seen the relationship. He had taken two giant steps away from the traditional view of doctor and patient. First, he had recognized that the nature of the relationship could facilitate or inhibit the analysis and that the analyst had some power to determine which of those effects it did indeed have. Second, he realized that an important part of the work of analysis could be done on the subject of the relationship itself.

Previously he had encouraged the working through by showing the patient how responses to early experiences shaped area after area of later life ("Can you see that you *expect* your teachers to be angry at you because of the old guilt you carry everywhere?"); now Freud was learning to add a new opportunity for understanding by showing the patient how the relationship with the therapist was shaped by those same responses. Psychoanalysis itself was an important event to the patient, and the analyst had now become an important person. All the usual responses and all the typical distortions of the patient's life would be bound to show up in relation to the therapist. This transference would enable the therapist to demonstrate convincingly to the patient how early fantasies and impulses distort contemporary reality. Whatever interfered with the patient's life would show up clearly in the transference, so why not use the transference to help the patient see the distortions? Since the therapist had the data right there before them, wouldn't that strategy make the learning all the more persuasive?

In his *Outline of Psychoanalysis* Freud says:

> It is the analyst's task constantly to tear the patient out of his . . . illusion [of the transference] and to show him again and again that what he takes to be new real life is a reflection of the past. . . . Careful handling of the transference . . . is as a rule richly rewarded. If we succeed, as we usually can, in enlightening the patient on the true nature of the phenomenon of transference, we shall have struck a powerful weapon out of the hand of his resistance and shall have converted dangers into gains. *For a patient never forgets again what he has experienced in the form of transference; it carries a greater force of conviction than anything he can acquire in other ways.*[10]

So somewhere between the professors and the checkout clerks I began learning how much I distorted my relationship with my analyst. I thought she was angry at me; I thought she neither liked nor approved of me; I thought she was disgusted by my fantasies. Sometimes she succeeded in getting me to see that I had no grounds for those ideas, that they were the products of that same unconscious guilt that so colored everything in my mind. And, indeed, learning about my guilt in relation to her did affect me more deeply than did learning about the professors and the checkout clerks.

We have seen, then, that Freud had first hoped that mere recall of the early impulses and relationships would be enough to effect change. When that hope was disappointed, he went on to hope that repeated recall would be more helpful. It was more helpful, but still not effective enough. Finally he hoped that a more convincing recall—recall in the transference—would so persuade the patient that all of his or her relationships were being distorted that change would simply have to follow. To his ever-growing disappointment, that seemed not to be enough either. He was learning a great deal about the mind, and some patients were undoubtedly being helped, but many were not.[11]

The theory of transference was a major discovery. The clinical relationship contains within it the whole story of the patient's problems, indeed the whole story of the patient's life. It is an astonishing microcosm. And it lays before the therapist a remarkable opportunity, not only for learning the secrets of the human mind but for helping the patient as well. It was puzzling and painful to Freud that he had not found the way to extract the full potential from this opportunity.

As we follow the history of the post-Freudian work with transference, it will be helpful to keep two things in mind. First, Freud believed therapy was effected by *remembering*, by recalling the early material and realizing how it affected one's present life. Second, Freud saw transference primarily as *distortion*, and he believed that by showing patients those distortions he could help them see the distortions throughout their lives.

Freud's work had made the greatest advances in the history of the field, but he had by no means solved all the problems. In later chapters we will see how Gill and Kohut, two of the most imaginative among his followers, have learned to use the phenomenon of transference to develop a more effective clinical relationship.

For many years psychoanalysis was the only significant force in American clinical practice, until an American psychologist named Carl Rogers arrived on the scene. His contribution to our understanding of the relationship between therapist and client was so monumental and influential that it will be worth our while to look at his work before we turn to Gill and Kohut.

3

The Influence of the Humanists

CARL ROGERS

∽

I first read Carl Rogers' books in the 1950s when, as a graduate student, I was immersed in the complex and fascinating world of academic psychology and the poetic vision of psychoanalysis. I found little to interest me in Rogers' writing. He was an American psychologist who believed the important parts of the mind were readily available to consciousness, he was cheerfully optimistic, and he seemed to have a predictable distaste for the dark aspects of European psychology. I thought he was mostly of historical interest.

Many years later, preparing a course, I set about rereading Rogers. I was utterly astonished. The simplicity of his view of the clinical relationship, which previously had seemed so naive to me, now seemed to have profound beauty and importance.

The therapy I will propose is quite different from the one Rogers practiced and taught. But it seems to me that whatever view one holds of the human mind and however

one chooses to conduct therapy, there is much to be
learned by paying careful attention to Rogers' advice
about the relationship between therapist and client.

Rogers' Great Influence

If I was not taken with Rogers' ideas when I first came
across them, the same could not be said for the field of
American clinical psychology. It would be an exaggeration
to claim that the publication of Carl Rogers' *Counseling
and Psychotherapy* in 1942[1] had the impact of, say, Freud's
Interpretation of Dreams, since Freud's books forever
changed not only the practice of psychotherapy but also
human beings' view of themselves. But if we exclude those
by Freud, it is hard to name another set of books that has
had an impact on clinical practice equal to Rogers'.

For a significant portion of the Western world's psychotherapists Rogers has legitimized the therapist's concern about the quality of the relationship between therapist
and client; indeed, he has made that quality the therapist's paramount concern. Freud offered a radical new
view of the mind, and drew from this view a set of remarkable inferences about how neurosis might be treated. The
key word was *treated.* As we have seen, Freud was a physician, and he saw neurosis as an illness to be cured. Rogers
was not a physician, and he did not view emotional difficulties as an indication of an illness to be cured. He called
the people with whom he worked "clients" rather than
"patients." He had at one time planned on being a minis-
ter, and though he abandoned that career, his religious
predilection can be seen in his view of psychology. He
believed that human beings need to be loved, and when
their need is inadequately met, the result is confusion
and pain. If someone could give the suffering person a

significant experience of the love so sorely missing, the confusion and pain would go away by itself.

A Therapy of Love

Rogers seldom said he was offering a therapy of love, and his way of helping people change was certainly different from the sentimentality that characterizes some New Age therapists. But I think it will help our understanding of his monumental contribution to our field to realize that he was indeed introducing into it the variable of love.

By "love" Rogers meant what the Greeks called "agape." Greek philosophy distinguished between two kinds of love, eros and agape. Eros is characterized by the desire for something that will fulfill the lover. It includes the wish to possess the beloved object or person. Agape, by contrast, is characterized by the desire to fulfill the beloved. It demands nothing in return and wants only the growth and fulfillment of the loved one. Agape is a strengthening love, a love that, by definition, does not burden or obligate the loved one.

Rogers spent forty years developing his view of therapy. And perhaps it would not be far off the mark to view his whole forty years' work as an attempt to shape an answer to a single question: What should a therapist do to convey to a client that at last he or she is loved?

To answer that question, Rogers and his students spent countless hours studying the process of psychotherapy. He was the first to make audio recordings of sessions and permit them to be studied and analyzed. He believed that therapy could be studied scientifically and continually improved by that research.[2]

Although Rogers developed a well-articulated theory of personality, he came to believe that it didn't matter what theory of personality you held. If the therapist successfully communicated the experience of agape, the client would change in the desired direction. Not only didn't the theory matter, neither did the technique. You could practice the nondirective, client-centered reflection that Rogers had developed in earlier years, or you could interpret free associations in the classic psychoanalytic manner, do Gestalt exercises, or analyze the transference. It didn't matter. Whatever suited the theory and style of the therapist was fine as long as agape was successfully communicated.[3]

What did matter, and it mattered considerably, was how agape was communicated. Rogers and his students had studied the problem assiduously for many years, and Rogers believed he knew what worked and what didn't. What he thought worked was a therapy that communicated to the client *genuineness, empathy,* and *unconditional positive regard.* Let's look at each of those concepts in detail.

Genuineness

Therapists must be *genuine.* That means they must have ongoing access to their own internal process, their own feelings, their own attitudes, and their own moods. Rogers believed that therapists who were not receptive to the awareness of their own flow of feeling and thought would be unlikely to help clients become aware of theirs. Undoubtedly there are therapists who choose this profession because they imagine that focusing on the client's internal process is a good way to avoid the pain and anxiety of looking at their own. Rogers teaches that this is a recipe for disaster. To become a therapist is to take on an awesome responsibility for facing oneself. Certainly the early psychoanalysts had understood this, though this understanding was sometimes only a peripheral aspect of their orientation, and too often it disappeared altogether. Rogers insisted on its being central.

To be aware of one's thoughts and feelings is not enough; therapists must do nothing to conceal this inner process from the client. They must not be defensive, but rather must be *transparent*. It is important to note that this concept implies nothing at all about what therapists are to say or do. It only suggests that they are to present themselves transparently, concealing nothing. They may do so silently, revealing their inner qualities in their eyes, facial expressions, and posture. Or they may choose sometimes to tell a client what they are feeling.

Rogers confesses he is not at all sure just how much therapists ought actually to say to clients about their own feelings or attitudes. He is quite sure that genuineness does not require anyone to blurt out every passing feeling. He is not, therefore, suggesting a form of encounter therapy, in which the therapist shares every feeling with the client. He thinks that genuineness perhaps calls for the therapist to express a feeling only when it has persisted and when it seems to be interfering with the therapist's ability to be fully present for the client. And then the feeling is to be presented carefully, with warmth, empathy, and full respect for the client. Let me quote here one of Rogers' examples:

> But is it always helpful to be genuine? What about negative feelings? What about the times when the counselor's real feeling toward the client is one of annoyance or boredom or dislike? My tentative answer is that even with such feelings as these, which we all have from time to time, it is preferable for the counselor to be real than to put up a facade of interest and concern and liking, which he does not feel.

But it is not a simple thing to achieve such reality. Being real involves the difficult task of being acquainted with the flow of experiencing going on within oneself, a flow marked especially by complexity and continuous change. So if I sense that I am feeling bored by my contacts with this [client], and this feeling persists, I think I owe it to him and to our relationship to share this feeling with him. But here again I will want to be constantly in touch with what is going on in me. I will recognize that it is *my* feeling of being bored which I am expressing, and not some supposed fact about him as a boring person. If I voice it as *my own* reaction, it has the potentiality of leading to a deeper relationship. But this feeling exists in the context of a complex and changing flow, and this needs to be communicated too. I would like to share with him my distress at feeling bored, and the discomfort I feel in expressing this aspect of me. As I share these attitudes I find that my feeling of boredom arises from my sense of remoteness from him, and that I would like to be more in touch with him. And even as I try to express these feelings, they change. I am certainly not bored as I try to communicate myself to him in this way, and I am far from bored as I wait with eagerness and perhaps a bit of apprehension for his response. I also feel a new sensitivity to him, now that I have shared this feeling which has been a barrier between us. So I am very much more able to hear the surprise or perhaps the hurt in his voice as he now finds *himself* speaking more genuinely because I have dared to be real with him. I have let myself be a person—real, imperfect—in my relationship with him.[4]

Rogers cautions therapists against using this sort of advice as a license to work out their own issues on the client's time, and he reminds his readers that often the appropriate person with whom to share their feelings is a supervisor or colleague, not the client.

In spite of the amount of time and energy Rogers devoted to writing about genuineness (he wrote about it in article after article), he seemed to find this attribute hard to describe and to illustrate. But it seems clear that intuitively he knew what he meant. At some level we all recognize when we are face to face with a person who is being genuine with us and when we are with someone who is putting on a polite or professional facade. With the former we feel trust and willingness to expose ourselves. It is this quality Rogers was trying to describe.

Rogers thought genuineness the most important attribute of all.

Empathy

The second condition essential to successful therapy is *empathy*. The dictionary meaning of *empathy* is the imaginative entering of another person's subjective experience. Rogers is talking about the importance of the therapist's continual attempt to understand the client's experience *from the client's point of view*. To Rogers, empathy is not merely cognitive; it also has an emotional, experiential component. To have empathy is to experience the client's world the way the client experiences it, but to experience it without getting lost in it, without ever losing the "as if" quality.

Whether the client is experiencing fear or uncertainty, loneliness or anger, admiration or disappointment, the empathic therapist makes every effort to experience what the client is experiencing and to communicate that understanding and experience to the client:

> "It must be very frightening to be so uncertain about your job security. And I also imagine you must be pretty angry at your boss."

> "I think I see what you're saying. In some ways you like coming here and talking to me, but you're not sure it's really doing very much for you."

"My goodness, you really love her, don't you?"

Rogers puts it like this:

> To sense [the client's] confusion or his timidity or his anger or his feeling of being treated unfairly as if it were your own, yet without your own uncertainty or fear or anger or suspicion getting bound up in it, this is the condition I am endeavoring to describe. When the client's world is clear to the counselor and she can move about in it freely, then she can both communicate her understanding of what is vaguely known to the client, and she can also voice meanings in the client's experience of which the client is scarcely aware.[5]

Two of Rogers' students, Charles Truax and Robert Carkhuff, describe the empathic therapist.[6] Here is a somewhat simplified summary:

Empathic therapists:

Have a manner and tone that indicate they take this relationship seriously.

Are aware of what the client is feeling now.

Have a capacity to communicate this understanding in a language attuned to those current feelings.

Make their comments in a way that fits with the client's mood and content. These comments indicate sensitive understanding of feelings the client has actually expressed and also serve to clarify and expand the client's awareness of feelings and experiences, including those of which the client is only partly aware.

Are able to stay in tune with the client's shifting emotional content so that they can correct themselves when they discover that their understanding and their comments have been off target. They are sensitive to their mistakes and do not cling to them, but easily and nondefensively change their response in midstream.

Continually give the client the message "I am with you."

Unfortunately, this sort of understanding is rare in our ordinary lives. It doesn't often happen that parent or teacher, friend or lover really tries to grasp what a given experience is like for us or that we try to grasp what one is like for them. In everyday life the understanding we tend to give and receive is some form of "I understand what makes you act that way" or "I understand what's wrong with you." Traditionally much of clinical understanding has taken this form:

"I think you're actually very angry at women."

"Perhaps you're focusing so much on my inadequacies in order to avoid looking at your feelings about this matter."

To Rogers this sort of thing isn't understanding at all; it's evaluation and analysis. It's viewing other people's lives in our terms, not in theirs.

The therapeutic value of *empathic* understanding seems clear: When I really comprehend that my therapist is trying to see my world the way I see it, I feel encouraged to clarify and therefore increase my understanding of myself. This empathy teaches me to be empathic with myself, to try gently to grasp my experience in the accepting way my therapist grasps it. And like all agape, another person's empathy has a crucial effect on my self-esteem. If my therapist thinks it worth the time and effort to try to understand my experience, I must be worth the time and effort.

Unconditional positive regard

The third necessary quality of the effective therapist is *unconditional positive regard*. Rogers takes the position that if I'm not on your side, *really* on your side, I have no business being in a therapy office with you. His model for this attribute is the loving parent who "prizes" the child. Such a parent has strong positive feelings for the child, feelings that are not possessive and do not demand that the child be a certain way. The parent gives the message that even though from time to time the child is likely to evoke annoyance, anger, disapproval, or disgust, the child is basically, essentially loved and lovable, no matter what. Similarly, a client may (and almost certainly will) reveal feelings and behaviors that clash with the therapist's values or aesthetics. Successful therapy depends on the therapist's ability at such times to keep in view the fact that clients are worthwhile human beings struggling gamely to find their way back to their birthright of growth and self-development, and as such they should be prized.

In Rogers' view it is important that this feeling be neither paternalistic nor sentimental, and that it give the client a great deal of room to be a separate and independent person.

If I go to a surgeon with a physical problem, the surgeon may not like me or even have any respect for me. I may find the situation a bit unpleasant, but if the surgeon is skilled and responsible, I will probably come out about as well as I would have if I had been prized. Rogers taught that the view of psychotherapy as analogous to surgery has led to serious difficulties in the practice of therapy and the training of therapists. We are not *doing* therapy, the way the surgeon does surgery; we *are* the therapy, and without a substantial amount of unconditional positive regard, we will not be successful.

Few of us had parents capable of that kind of unconditional prizing. Many of us learned that we were loved only when we did something or revealed some feeling that pleased our parents. It might be something convenient for them, or nonthreatening to them, or something they could be proud of. Many of our feelings, wishes, and impulses did not fit the category of "pleasing to our parents." We quickly learned that those feelings and impulses were unlovable, and it was a short step to the belief that they were *bad*. It is easy to understand how we then lost touch with our deepest nature:

> If I have been taught that to be lovable I must harbor only good feelings and good impulses,

> And if I have become convinced that my true self is full of bad feelings and bad impulses,

> Then I will set about trying to disavow the parts of me about which I have such gloomy suspicions.

If a goal of the therapist is to make it safe for clients to explore their deepest nature, we can see why Rogers thought that unconditional positive regard was essential.

The Three Attributes as Continua

Genuineness, empathy, and unconditional positive regard—these, then, are the three attributes that Rogers thought necessary to a successful clinical relationship. I'm sure it has occurred to you that if any of us could always be fully genuine, empathic, and warmly accepting, we would be in a state of nirvana or in heaven and not available to earthly clients. It had occurred to Rogers, too. He did not think that any mortal would ever be perfect in any of the three. Rather, he saw each of these attributes as a continuum and believed that the art of becoming a therapist consisted entirely in developing one's capacity to move farther and farther along each of those three continua. The farther along one was, the better therapist one would be.

The Implications of Rogers' Theory

The implications of this view are extraordinarily radical. Note the word *entirely* in the above paragraph. One implication of Rogers' view is that no special intellectual or professional knowledge is required of therapists or will do them the slightest good. Studying theories and techniques, however interesting they may be, is of no value to the therapist.[7] Training could be helpful, in fact very helpful, but that training would not consist of the acquisition of knowledge. It would be experiential training, the sort of training that would help therapists increase their self-awareness so that they might become more genuine in all aspects of their lives, sensitive to all the people they deal with, so that they might be more empathic with clients. And it would be a training that would enable them to come to terms with their buried prejudices and resentments so that they might be free to prize their clients.

As I have said, Rogers did not consider himself an encounter therapist; he didn't see it as appropriate to share every passing feeling with his clients. Yet in the early 1960s he began to spend more and more time leading encounter groups and sensitivity-training groups. He saw these groups as offering the sort of training that developed the attributes he thought essential to a therapist. He greatly regretted that almost nowhere was such sensitivity enhancement a part of the formal training of therapists.[8]

Another radical implication of Rogers' view is that there is no therapeutic value in diagnosis.[9] That is, finding a category into which the client may be fitted adds nothing to the therapist's effectiveness. It doesn't make any difference whether you think your client is borderline or narcissistic or schizophrenic or mildly depressed. If you can be genuine, if you can communicate that you are managing to grasp your clients' experiences, and if you can let them know of your unshakable regard for their worth as human beings—if you can do all that to a significant degree, then your clients will grow and change, whatever label might be applied to them. (Rogers did come to believe that clients who were not motivated to change were hard to work with and unlikely to change very much. He found that many people diagnosed as schizophrenic were unmotivated to change—as were a lot of people not so diagnosed.)

Rogers' idea about the components of successful therapy clearly implies a certain philosophical attitude. Rogers believed the purpose of life is "to be that which one truly is."[10] Our clients are in trouble because they have been successfully taught that it is not acceptable to be what they truly are. Thus Rogers asked therapists to do their best to listen as carefully as possible in order to find out who the client truly is. As the therapist carefully attends, the client gradually learns that it is all right to be whoever he or she truly is, and since Rogers believed that being one's true self is the purpose of life, it is easy to see why he thought self-acceptance is the most valuable thing a therapist can give a client.

Rogers believed that in order to find their work useful, therapists probably ought to hold a philosophical position similar to his own.[11] If you do not, you are likely to try to guide clients into being what *you* think they ought to be. Rogers believed that some therapists' attitudes simply do not mesh with the view he was offering. Some examples of those incompatible attitudes:

> People are neither valuable nor unvaluable; they are simply interesting to try to figure out.

> They may not even be particularly interesting, but they furnish material for books and articles, which is to say for ideas, and ideas certainly *are* interesting.

> The therapist soon learns all there is of interest to learn about the client. The rest of the work consists of getting the client to learn it.

> The therapist's theory handles all the data. When enough knowledge has been gathered, the client will fit the theory.

> Clients can't be trusted to find their own way. If they're left to their own devices, they will resist, defend, and do whatever they can to impede change and growth. The therapist's job is to protect the client against those self-destructive tendencies.

That is, the therapist knows better than the clients what is good for them and tries to figure out a way to influence them for their own good.

But if the therapist believes in the essential worth of the individual, if the context in which the therapist works is great respect for the person and the person's potentialities, then, Rogers thought, that therapist will find the attributes of genuineness, empathy, and warm acceptance congenial, natural, and altogether understandable.

Rogers' Optimal Therapy

In 1961 Rogers offered a description of what he thought therapy was like at its best:

> If the therapy were optimal, intensive as well as extensive, then it would mean that the therapist has been able to enter into an intensely personal and subjective relationship with the client—relating not as a scientist to an object of study, not as a physician expecting to diagnose and cure, but as a person to a person. It would mean that the therapist feels this client to be a person of unconditional self-worth: of value no matter what his condition, his behavior, or his feelings. It would mean that the therapist is genuine, hiding behind no defensive façade, but meeting the client with the feelings which organically he is experiencing. It would mean that the therapist is able to let himself go in understanding this client; that no inner barriers keep him from sensing what it feels like to be the client at each moment of the relationship; and that he can convey something of his empathic understanding to the client. It means that the therapist has been comfortable in entering this relationship fully, without knowing cognitively where it will lead, satisfied with providing a climate which will permit the client the utmost freedom to become himself.
>
> For the client, the optimal therapy would mean an exploration of increasingly strange and unknown and dangerous feelings in himself, the exploration proving possible only because he is gradually realizing that he is accepted unconditionally. Thus he becomes acquainted with elements of his experience which have in the past been denied to awareness as too threatening, too damaging to the structure of the self. He finds himself experiencing these feelings fully, completely, in the relationship, so that for the moment he is his fear, or

his anger, or his tenderness, or his strength. And as he lives these widely varied feelings, in all their degrees of intensity, he discovers that he has experienced *himself*, that he *is* all these feelings. He finds his behavior changing in a constructive fashion in accordance with his newly experienced self. He approaches the realization that he no longer needs to fear what experience may hold, but can welcome it freely as a part of his changing and developing self.[12]

④

A Re-experiencing Therapy

MERTON GILL

∽

Merton Gill, M.D. (1914-1944), was a long time member of the psychoanalytic establishment and one of its most eminent. Few members of that community have thought so deeply or written so influentially about the clinical relationship as Merton Gill.[1] Gill said quite explicitly that his views on the clinical relationship pertain not merely to psychoanalysis but to all forms of psychodynamic therapy, including the kinds that are offered once or twice a week.[2]

What About Therapy Is Therapeutic?

Remembering . . . ?

Perhaps the best way to understand Gill's contribution to our topic is to wonder for a moment what about therapy is therapeutic. To Freud, a cure comes about from the patient's *remembering* thoughts and feelings long repressed. To understand that idea, it might be helpful to review a few basic elements of Freud's theory of psychopathology.

To Freud, we are the species who represses ourselves. Our fate is to be caught in intense, persistent conflict. Regardless of what the socializing community does or doesn't do, conflicts arise from human nature itself. Mental life is driven by powerful instincts; these instincts clash with one another, and they clash with the reality constraints of the outside world.[3] And before a child is very old, he or she has a sizable collection of fears, something else for the instincts to clash with. Thus conflict is everywhere. When one of these conflicts becomes sufficiently intense, it becomes too painful to keep in awareness, and so it is repressed; that is, it is relegated to the realm of unconsciousness. This is a successful short-term solution to the problem of painful awareness, and in modest doses it's an adaptive long-term solution as well. Our mental life would be unacceptably chaotic without a moderate amount of repression. Excessive repression, however, has serious long-term consequences:

1. It takes a significant amount of psychic energy to keep an impulse repressed. That energy is not available for living one's life.

2. Repressed material is by definition unconscious and therefore not under the control of the conscious, rational faculties; that is, it's not under the control of that part of the mind Freud called the ego. Thus it may cause all sorts of trouble. We saw several instances of this kind of trouble in Chapter 2, in our examination of the repetition compulsion.

3. Repressed material acts as a magnet, drawing other impulses into the unconscious. If I have passionate impulses toward my mother, it is healthy and adaptive

for me to repress them. But if that area of repression spreads to include passionate impulses toward all women, my life will be difficult indeed.

Freud believed that it was excessive repression that created problems for his patients. Their lives were being manipulated by inner forces of which they were unaware and which they therefore could not control. As we saw in Chapter 2, Freud hoped that if he could make the repressed material conscious, and if that new consciousness could somehow be emotionally utilized—that is, made an effective part of the patient's awareness—the problems would lessen. In other words, he wanted his patients to remember, and to remember with conviction.[4]

Imagine a man who suffers from an inability to experience both passionate and tender feelings toward the same woman. He may feel passionate toward one sort of woman and tender toward another, but he can't feel both toward any one woman. Freud would say that the man had repressed early impulses and memories related to conflicting feelings of desire and fear—desire for his mother and fear of punishment for those desires. Thus when he feels tender toward a woman, he categorizes her "like mother." If he experiences passionate feelings toward her, he unconsciously sees them as incestuous and forbidden. Freud believed that if the man could recapture the memory of those feelings and the events associated with them and work through those memories, the problem would be significantly lessened. This is *remembering* therapy.

Freud set himself two goals when he was working with a patient. One was to ease her neurotic suffering; the other was to use the information he gleaned from her to help construct a theory of the mind. To the end of his life he believed that these two tasks not only were compatible but were the same. That is, he believed that the truth would make his patients free. If he could unearth the secrets of this patient's unconscious, if he could absolutely convince her that this hidden story was the root of her suffering, then her expanded knowledge would perform the therapeutic transformation. And Freud believed that as he learned this patient's hidden story, he would be simultaneously learning the hidden story of humankind. Beneath the façade of human consciousness lay an amazing puzzle, a captivating mystery. And the patient's buried story contained the ingredients of the solution.

Ever since, psychoanalysis has attracted practitioners who are puzzle solvers, therapists who want to get to the bottom of the mystery and who share Freud's belief that this fascination with the puzzles of psychic life is in the patient's best interest.

Gill is one of a growing number of modern psychoanalysts who, though they find a great deal of Freud's work indispensable, no longer believe that uncovering the hidden story is enough to liberate the client. For generations now, with client after client, psychoanalysts have succeeded in unearthing the unconscious fantasies that give rise to symptoms and have succeeded in convincingly communicating this analysis to their clients, but in a discouraging number of cases the symptoms remain. The clients have remembered the old impulses and the old fears. But remembering has not been enough.

. . . Or re-experiencing?

Gill and like-minded colleagues accept Freud's theory of psychopathology, and although they believe that remembering is necessary to effect significant change in therapy, they find that it is not sufficient. Actually, Freud himself had doubts as to whether remembering was sufficient. Though his published clinical work indicates his unflagging commitment to the recapturing of lost memories, there are places in his theoretical writings where one can find the basis for re-experiencing therapy. One of many examples:

> . . . the whole of the patient's illness . . . is concentrated on a single point—his relation to the doctor. . . . When the transference has risen to this significance, work upon the patient's memories retreats far into the background. Thereafter it is not incorrect to say that we are no longer concerned with the patient's earlier illness but with a newly created and transformed neurosis which has taken the former's place.[5]

If remembering is not enough, what is missing is *re-experiencing*. Gill believes that because the client's difficulties were acquired through experience, they must be transformed through experience. They cannot be reasoned away. While it is necessary for clients eventually to understand the roots of their difficulties, that understanding cannot be merely delivered as an explanation. It must emerge as clients re-experience certain aspects of their past. And this re-experiencing must occur within the therapeutic relationship. Gill says:

> The transference is primarily a result of the patient's efforts to realize his wishes, and the therapeutic gain results primarily from re-experiencing these wishes in the transference, realizing that they are significantly determined by something pre-existing within the patient, and experiencing something new in examining them together with the analyst—the one to whom the wishes are now directed.[6]

Thus a re-experiencing therapist believes that the client must have an opportunity to relive emotionally the impulses, the anxieties, and the conflicts of his past and to relive them under certain specified conditions.

Conditions for Therapeutic Re-experiencing

According to Gill, if re-experiencing is to be therapeutic, the impulses, feelings, and expectations must be experienced under the following conditions:

1. They must be experienced in the presence of the person toward whom they are now directed.

2. The re-experienced feelings must be *expressed* toward the person toward whom they are now directed. It is not enough for the client merely to experience the feelings silently.

So far, it seems that it should be therapeutic for the old feelings to be re-experienced toward anyone, as long as they are expressed to that person. But now we come to the next condition:

3. The new object of the old feelings and expectations, the person toward whom they are now directed, must be willing, even determined, to discuss the client's feelings and impulses with interest, objectivity, and without defensiveness.

According to Gill, this condition is absolutely essential to the therapeutic process. Given the low probability of encountering such a response in our ordinary lives, we begin to see why Gill views the therapeutic situation as a unique opportunity.

4. The client must be helped to learn the ancient and deep source of the re-experienced impulses. Thus remembering and re-experiencing become organically blended.

So Freud's troubled patient who cannot combine love and desire will sooner or later find himself experiencing toward the therapist (irrespective of whether the therapist is a man or a woman) impulses he considers forbidden. As we saw in Chapter 2, this is what the repetition compulsion demands.

If the therapist:

Helps the client get in touch with these feelings,

Makes it safe for the client to express them,

Discusses these feelings with the client in a nonjudgmental, nondefensive, interested fashion,

And eventually, when the therapy has progressed far enough, helps the client learn the ancient roots of these feelings,

then Gill's conditions for therapeutic re-experiencing have been met.

It is worth noting here that it is not only modern psychoanalysts who have come to believe that figuring out the cause of the symptom is not enough. Most schools of therapy hold some version of this belief, and each school has its own idea of what must be added to the insight. Many psychologists who are not therapists would agree. Psychologists who study the laws of learning think about it this way: In the learning laboratory the easiest way to get an animal or a person to unlearn an old response is to recreate the situation in which that response was originally learned. In fact, it can be hard to get someone to unlearn a response if you don't recreate the old situation. Freud's patient has learned the response of sexual inhibition to the stimulus of a "motherlike" woman. The learning psychologist would see this patient as needing to unlearn that response and learn a new one—one that better suits his present needs. The psychologist would doubt that it would do much good merely to explain to the patient how he came to acquire the old response. Therapists of many persuasions would agree. A cognitive-behavioral therapist, for example, would say that the patient had learned a faulty cognition.[7] The true state of affairs is that it is forbidden to feel passionate toward one's mother, but it is lawful and laudable to feel passionate toward other "nice" women, particularly nice women of the appropriate age. The faulty cognition the patient had acquired is that it is forbidden to feel passionate toward any "nice" woman. The therapist would give the patient repeated opportunities to rehearse the faulty cognition. The rehearsals would bring it into consciousness and recreate a crucial aspect of the original destructive learning. Then the therapist would be in a position to teach the client repeatedly to rehearse the appropriate thought: "I was mistaken; it's perfectly OK to feel passionate toward a nice woman."

To many modern psychoanalysts, including Gill, the optimal place for the re-experiencing is the relationship with the therapist.

A New Importance Seen in Transference

The emphasis on re-experiencing represents an important change in the psychoanalytic view of transference. To Freud, the value of transference lay in its power to help the patient remember, and to remember with conviction. To

Gill, the value of transference lies in providing the client a chance to experience once more the old feelings and expectations. The response to the original expression of those feelings generated the pain and confusion that eventually brought the client to the therapist. As the feelings are re-experienced in the transference, now directed at the person of the therapist, they will evoke a significantly different response. To Gill, this is the main therapeutic opportunity provided by the phenomenon of transference. This view of therapy implies that it is to clients' advantage to be more and more closely in touch with their experience of the therapist and of the relationship. This experience includes their

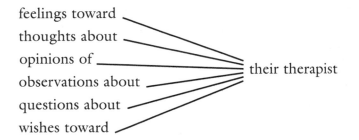

feelings toward
thoughts about
opinions of
observations about
questions about
wishes toward

their therapist

and, just as important, the feelings, thoughts, opinions, observations, questions, and wishes that clients believe the therapist has about them.

The Inevitability of Resistance

It is understandably frightening for the client to contemplate experiencing, let alone expressing, any but the mildest and safest feelings toward the therapist. It is not easy to tell *anyone* our feelings, impressions, or fantasies about him or her. And it is much harder when we are depending on that person for significant help. When we recall that this developing relationship with the therapist carries with it more and more unconscious reminders of our earliest and most difficult times, we can understand a client's determination to resist all aspects of transference—experiencing it, revealing it, learning its roots. And finally, a great deal of experience has taught the client that people are seldom eager to hear about one's feelings toward them. The client, Gill notes, will assume that the therapist would rather not be burdened by such a confession, and much of the time that assumption will be correct. However strong the therapist's theoretical belief about the value of learning the client's feelings about him or her, the therapist will inevitably feel as much resistance as the client does, and the client will not have much difficulty detecting it.

Clients inevitably have reactions to the therapist's behaviors and personal attributes, and if the situation is made sufficiently safe, they will reveal them. Not all of these reactions will be congruent with the therapist's self-image, and the therapist will need to be remarkably open to these reactions and accept them gracefully when they come.

The therapist's most important and delicate job is to help the client through this resistance, so that the client's awareness of thoughts and feelings about the therapist, however subtle and however disguised, may continually increase. We can see how important this step is to a re-experiencing therapist.[8]

Decoding the Transference

To help clients become aware of their relationship with the therapist, the therapist must first be sensitive to the fact that, given these resistances, allusions to the therapeutic situation are likely to be *encoded*, often as references to other situations. Second, from moment to moment, the therapist must be sensitive to what is going on in the therapeutic situation in order to have some idea what stimuli the client is responding to. Gill has completely abandoned the old assumption that the therapist is a blank screen. Who the therapist is and what the therapist does are very likely to be major causes of the client's responses. If the client talks about feeling criticized on the job, the therapist will scan recent events in the therapy to see whether any of them may have made the client feel criticized. If that scan turns up a possibility, the therapist sets out to decode, as tactfully and respectfully as possible, the client's statement about the situation.

Gill places great emphasis on tact and respect, reminding us that clients say what they mean, and what they say is of great importance to them. Gill hopes that a therapist would not say, "What you mean is that you feel criticized by me" or "What you are really saying is that you feel criticized by me." The client neither said nor meant that. Rather, a sensitive therapist might say, "I can understand that feeling criticized at work is very disturbing to you. And I wonder if an additional meaning of what you say is that in our last session you felt criticized by me."[9]

To the re-experiencing school of psychoanalysts, the relationship is central; it is what makes the re-experiencing possible. As the therapist encourages awareness of the client's experience of the relationship, clients become more aware of their shifting and developing attitudes toward the therapist. In addition, that relationship assumes greater and greater importance to them. Thus the relationship becomes the microcosm of their lives—their confusions, their ways of relating, their longings and disappointments, hopes and frustrations. During the therapeutic hour, after all, all other relationships are abstract, are at a distance. Only the therapeutic relationship is right there in the room and thus available for exploration with a unique depth, immediacy, and power.

Gill recognizes that it is very important to discuss the client's earlier life, as well as his or her present life outside the therapeutic situation. But he also believes that the most power of all is to be found in the client's talk about the relationship with the therapist. And so this question arises: Is it true that so much of what the client says really pertains to the therapist? Gill would respond: Whether or not it's true, it is *useful* to operate on that assumption. In any case, Gill's experience leads him to say yes, it is true.

Since encouraging awareness of the relationship is so important in Gill's system, let's look at some examples:

> 1. Often the transference is coded as being about a relationship with another person: "I'm starting to trust my lover a bit more, I think." The therapist will acknowledge that this is an important change in the client's life and give the topic as much time and attention as seems useful. Later, at an appropriate time, the therapist will look for a graceful opportunity to add: "I'm aware that we had a good session last week. I wonder if an additional meaning of what you say about your lover is that you're starting to have more trust in me."

> Another client's complaint that his wife makes unreasonable demands on him may remind the therapist that he and the client recently had to negotiate an appointment time, and he may wonder aloud if the client has found *him* demanding and unreasonable.[10]

> 2. Sometimes the transference is coded as being about another situation: "I went to a party last night, and the atmosphere was so heavy and depressing." The

therapist will convey understanding of how that experience must have felt, and then, when it seems plausible to do so, will say, "Your talking about the party last night raises another question. We've been having difficult sessions lately, and I wonder if you're finding the atmosphere in here a bit heavy as well."

3. The transference may also be coded as an expression of concern about how another person feels about the client: "I really want to know how my boss feels about me. I can't stand this uncertainty." The therapist will acknowledge how difficult that uncertainty must be, and after the discussion about the boss may say, "Is it possible that you also have some questions about how I feel about you?"

A common sequence is an initial glancing reference to the therapy situation followed by a description of a relationship or situation outside the therapy.[11] The client says:

"That was a good session last week. (*pause*) I'm starting to trust my lover a bit more, I think."

"I really didn't want to come in today. (*pause*) I went to a party last night, and the atmosphere was so heavy and depressing."

"I was thinking this week that I talk a lot more in here than you do. (*pause*) I really want to know how my boss feels about me. I can't stand this uncertainty."

In these instances the therapist's job is made easier, because the plausibility of the interpretation is enhanced by the client's tangential reference to the transference.

Liberating the Therapist's Warmth and Spontaneity

The classic view of psychoanalysis was that all of the cues of the analytic environment should be as neutral as the analyst. The physical environment should send the client no definite messages about the person who furnished and inhabits this office. The analyst should be silent, noncommittal, and nonresponsive. Above all, there should be no clue as to the personality or the values of the analyst. As we have seen, the absence of cues was intended to provide a blank screen onto which clients could project their transferences, uncontaminated by reality.

To Gill, this is not neutrality at all. Someone who says neither hello nor good-bye, who doesn't answer questions, who remains silent under severe provocation, is hardly neutral. When one feels cold and lonely with such a person, Gill says, it shouldn't be assumed that these feelings come from one's childhood. Who *wouldn't* feel cold and lonely in the face of that kind of treatment?

This observation raises an important issue. Psychoanalysts regularly observe that the analytic situation produces a considerable amount of regressed transference material: clients experience themselves as very young and as occupied with primitive needs. A client may, for instance, feel like a starving baby, begging for nurturance. At such times it is commonly assumed that the analysis has revealed something deep and important about the client's history—that long ago the client actually felt that way. Undoubtedly that is often the case. But it seems likely that sometimes this material is not revealing the client's history at all but is actually being created by the excessively cold ambiance the analyst has created in pursuit of neutrality.[12]

Providing the client with a "blank screen" is manifestly impossible; the situation is going to be rife with clues no matter what I do as a therapist, so I might as well permit myself a good deal of spontaneity. This strategy not only will create a more therapeutic atmosphere but will liberate my own creativity. Thus some degree of spontaneity seems very much in the client's interest.

Such freedom carries with it responsibility: the responsibility to pay close attention to all the elements of the situation, including the things one does and the way one does them. The client's reactions will be strongly influenced by two things: (1) what is actually happening in therapy and (2) the expectations, needs, and attitude the client brings to the situation. It is important to recognize that the client's responses are determined by what the therapist does as well as by the forces of transference.

In seeing therapy as an *interpersonal* situation, Gill differs from the classical analysts, who tried hard to be nonpersons, who believed they had successfully created a blank screen, and who perhaps underestimated how much what they did and didn't do contributed to the client's experience. Just as a dream, Gill says, uses the events of the preceding day as opportunities to explore deep content, so the client will use elements of the therapeutic situation as material for elaborating the transference phenomena. It is an error to believe that therapy develops in a social vacuum. In Gill's view: "The therapist may deny that he is reacting to the patient, but it is impossible for him to avoid such reaction. . . . The therapist who does not recognize the inevitably social nature of the therapeutic situation is in the grip of the companion illusion to the illusion of himself as a blank screen. . . . It is the illusion that the patient is naive."[13]

Let's look at a couple of examples:

1. In a therapy session I inappropriately told my client, a physician, a story about my own life that I must somehow have thought was relevant. He smiled politely and didn't respond. Had I followed Gill's advice, I would have asked him how he felt about my having told that story. Gill urges us to give the client a lot of opportunities to respond to us. But I didn't ask, probably because I was starting to doubt the wisdom of having told the story. The session ended and the client got up to go. Before leaving, he told me a humorous story of his own: "I was working in the emergency room last night when these two drunks came in. One of them had hurt himself and was trying to explain the problem to me. His friend chimed in to help and the first drunk said to me, 'Don't pay any attention to him—he's as drunk as I am.'" I laughed uneasily as he left. At the next session I asked him if he had been made uncomfortable by the personal story I had told and if he was wondering who was watching the store. He agreed that was the case. I said perhaps his story about the emergency room was his way of letting me know that. He said he hadn't seen the connection at the time, but it did make sense.

2. A client who is not a particularly political type spends some minutes criticizing liberals; according to him, if they had their way, they'd give everything away to the poor. The therapist, who considers himself a liberal, is puzzled by remarks that seem out of character and out of context. How could they possibly be about him? Suddenly he catches sight of his overcoat hanging on the coatrack, with a political button on the lapel,

plain to see. Now he has an opening for investigating how the material relates to him.

Gill has some advice for the therapist who has not noticed the button. Were the therapist sufficiently puzzled by the political material, it would be altogether appropriate to say, "You know, I keep wondering if an additional meaning of what you are saying relates to me. Do you have some thoughts about my politics?" The client might then mention the button or merely say that he imagines most psychotherapists are liberals.

To repeat: There's no way, Gill says, to keep reality stimuli out of the situation. Thus it is important to stay aware of what those stimuli may be and be ready to recognize the client's references to them, no matter how coded those references may be. It is also important to inquire about the client's response whenever the therapist does something unusual. Within the limits of ethics, Gill says, no choice the therapist makes will be fatal if the client is encouraged to share his or her response to it.

Perhaps it is not necessary to add that this is one more aspect of therapy that requires a considerable amount of nondefensiveness. If I have made an obvious error, the defensive side of me hopes fervently that the client will overlook it. The client, no more eager to embarrass me than I am to be embarrassed, may try to cooperate. Nonetheless, it is likely that sooner or later a reference to my mistake will show up in the client's material. It is equally likely that it will be so well disguised that I could easily let it pass and allow my error to slip into oblivion. But I will be abandoning a therapeutic advantage if I do so. Not the least of this advantage is my opportunity to provide clients with what is probably the first relationship they have ever had in they and another person can discuss the other person's mistakes with the same interest and energy they bring to any other subject.

A therapist who acknowledges that he or she is not a blank screen, not a detached observer, unlocks the door to a vast realm. Gill understood the implications.[14] He opened the door and flung it wide, thus becoming one of the godfathers of an increasingly significant movement in psychoanalysis called *intersubjectivity* or *social constructivism*.[15] These terms refer to the understanding that, just as the client's conscious and unconscious responses affect the ongoing process, so do those of the therapist. There are two subjectivities in the consulting room. Each observes the actual data of the interaction and each interprets them in the light of ancient expectations and wishes. The classical analysts tried hard to be objective and in touch with reality. Someone, they thought, had to watch the store. The intersubjectivists have moved a long step away from that position, saying it is now clear that

1. Therapists exert significant unconscious influence on the interaction, influence they can learn about only from the client.

2. They must learn to be gently skeptical about their own objectivity and their own view of the client's reality.

Gill's close associate Irwin Hoffman has written extensively about these concepts, as has Robert Stolorow, a creative and imaginative student of Gill's work.[16] There are differences among the various authors, but the main thrust is clear. Here is how Gill talks about it:

Interpersonal experience is a resultant of how a person [inter-
prets] the behavior and . . . experience of the other and of his
behaving in a way designed to elicit confirmation of his prior
expectations. That is, he both interprets interactions and con-
structs or shapes them in particular ways. . . . Since interpretation and construction are always operative and always based
on [the person's] past as well as [on the] present [situation],
all interpersonal experience is transferential. . . . In any interpersonal relationship, the interlocking of the interpretation
and construction in which each participant engages, as well as
the unconscious and hence unknown factor in all human
motivation, makes it impossible to say what the relationship is
in some objective unequivocal sense and what is the contribution of each."[17]

It is crucial to note that Gill does not follow Freud in
thinking of transference as distortion.[18] He does indeed
agree with Freud's remarkable discovery that we carry
with us, as residua of our childhoods, unconscious expectations and unconscious needs that strongly affect the way
we see and respond to the contemporary world. But
whereas Freud went on to argue that often those needs
induce us to distort our perceptions in significant ways,
Gill thinks of these perceptions as perfectly reasonable in
the circumstances. Gill reasons that we are all continually
faced with the necessity of making inferences from inade-
quate data. We are all continually faced with ambiguous
stimuli and ambiguous situations that we must interpret.
We deal with these ambiguities by attempting to resolve
them in accordance with the unconscious needs and
expectations we have carried with us from childhood. We
are not distorting the world; we are trying to arrive at the
most plausible construction of it we can, given the ambiguities and given our history. That is an important aspect
of the intersubjective position.

We have now seen how strongly Gill stresses the need to help clients increase both their awareness of the relationship and their willingness to discuss it. As his career proceeded, he found himself placing more and more emphasis on those goals. But he has never lost sight of the other major goal of psychodynamic therapy: to help clients learn the ancient roots of their unconscious attitudes.

The Place of Remembering

If re-experiencing were the only goal, the therapist would only need to encourage an awareness of the relationship. But as we have seen, Gill also believes in (1) the importance of remembering and (2) transference as the royal road to that remembering. Just being aware of one's feelings toward the therapist, vitally important though it is, isn't enough. The client must also be helped to see that some part of those feelings is not entirely determined by the realities of the present situation. The remaining determinants are the attitudes, expectations, and needs the client brings to the consulting room. The more she realizes how those old forces affect her relationship with the therapist, the more clearly she will come to understand how they shape her whole life, and so, the less power those ancient forces will have.

Let me illustrate that aspect of transference analysis, and then let's see how Gill talks about it. I gave an illustration earlier:

> **Client:**   I was thinking this week that I talk a lot more in here than you do. (*pause*) I really want to know how my boss feels about me. I can't stand this uncertainty.

Gill would now be alerted to the possibility that, in addition to concern about the boss, there is a hidden allusion to the therapist. "That must be difficult." And when the opportunity occurs: "Is it possible that you also have some questions about how I feel about you?" If the client denies this possibility and continues to deny it after some gentle prompting, then either the decoding is incorrect or the resistance is not ready to yield. In that case, the therapist will accept the denial and let it pass. But surprisingly often, Gill suggests, the client accepts the therapist's interpretation:

Client: Well, I suppose I have been wondering about that. I mean you don't ever say. To tell you the truth, I've been thinking lately that you don't seem very interested in me.

Therapist: Can you say what gives you that impression?

Client: Not really. It's just an idea I had.

At this point Gill's thought process goes something like this: I do give her minimal cues, so it's reasonable she would be trying to figure out what I'm up to and how I feel about her. She has to come up with the most plausible hypothesis she can devise. The hypothesis that I don't reveal much because I'm not interested is certainly plausible. But the exchange between us has been spirited and quite warm for some weeks, so the situation doesn't seem ambiguous enough to account for the hypothesis that I'm not interested in her. So it's a safe bet that this is a valuable transference issue. If Gill judges this to be a point in the therapy where it is appropriate to help the client look at the transference aspects of the situation, he might do so this way:

Therapist: That's certainly a plausible idea. There are times when I don't talk very much in here, and that could lead you to wonder just how interested I am in you. (*pause*) On the other hand, it seems to me that we've had some warm interchanges recently. That makes me wonder if there aren't other ways you could possibly interpret my manner with you.

Client: I suppose there are.

Therapist: I wonder if there was an earlier time in your life when you feared that somebody important to you wasn't very interested in you.

Now the therapist is in a position to explore some of the client's early experiences and also help her see how those experiences influence her perceptions now.

Interpreting Resistance to the Recognition of Transference

The process illustrated in the last example Gill thinks of as *interpreting resistance to the recognition of transference*. Just as clients are likely to resist awareness of feelings about the therapist, so they are likely to resist seeing that those feelings are transference phenomena.[19] It is unsettling for us to learn that the determinants of our feelings and perceptions are not only what they seem, and so we tend to resist such discoveries. We are likely to resist them even more strongly when the hidden causes come from the most painful and frightening issues of our history. That is why Gill calls this step interpreting resistance. And he reminds us that if we suggest to clients that their perceptions are distorted, our interpretations are in danger of sounding critical and humiliating, and our clients are even more likely to resist them.

Gill suggests three ways in which we can interpret resistance to the recognition of transference: (1) here-and-now interpretation, (2) contemporary life interpretation, and (3) genetic interpretation.

Here-and-now interpretation

The here-and-now interpretation uses aspects of the therapy situation to help the client see that a particular response to the therapist is not as inevitable as it seems. These interpretations depend neither on the client's history nor on the client's life outside the therapy situation. Consider again the client who thinks the therapist isn't very interested in her. At first it seems to the client that her fears of the therapist's indifference are determined entirely by the realities of the current situation. The therapist reminds her of events in the therapy that she has overlooked to help her see that those realities are subject to other interpretations, and thus prepares the way for her to explore the determinants of transference.

I once appeared on my analyst's front porch in a snowstorm and found the screen door locked. I had been entering through that door and the wooden one behind it for many months and had never before found either of them locked. I finally had to ring the doorbell. Once on the couch, I complained bitterly about being locked out. My analyst knew for certain that the door had not been locked at all. Had she been as tactful as Gill, she might have said, "I can certainly understand your feeling terrible about being locked out in the bad weather, and it's plausible that I had locked the door, since you had trouble opening it. But perhaps there are other interpretations. Perhaps the door was just a bit stuck, and instead of forcing it open,

you took that opportunity to re-experience some old feelings. You often feel rejected by me." Though less tactful,
she did convey that message. I scoffed.

Upon leaving, 50 minutes later, I examined the door
carefully. Indeed, the frame had swollen in the wet
weather. Further, to my astonishment, there was no lock
on the door. At the next session I went seriously to work
on my readiness to feel rejected by her.

Contemporary life interpretation

Contemporary life interpretation helps the client see that
a particular attitude toward the analyst is similar to his
attitudes toward other people he deals with. When I complained about that "locked" door, my analyst might have
said (with complete accuracy), "Shouldn't we perhaps
look at how similar these feelings are to those you have
about your teachers and classmates? You often feel that
they don't 'let you in.'" I would have agreed, and she
might then have said, "So perhaps your interpretation of
the stuck door, though certainly plausible, was another
instance of those feelings of yours."

Similarly, in the case of the client who thought her therapist wasn't very interested in her, the therapist might
have said, "Isn't this the way you feel about many people
in your life? Perhaps . . ."

The idea, of course, is that if clients can see that their
feelings about the therapist are similar to feelings they
often have toward other people, they will come to see that
those feelings toward the therapist are in part transference.

Gill doesn't use contemporary life interpretations as
much as he does here-and-now ones. He reasons that he
can be most effective when the entire situation, including
his evidence for transference, is immediately available to
both himself and the client.

Genetic interpretation

The genetic interpretation helps the client see the similarity between feelings toward the therapist and feelings toward people in the client's past. The word *genetic* does not refer here to the influence of DNA on behavior; Gill uses it rather in the sense of "genesis"—that is, how these themes began in the client's life. Let's look at an example:

> **Therapist:** You sound very angry at me. (*The client is silent.*) Are you feeling angry at me today?
>
> **Client:** Yes, as a matter of fact, I am kind of angry. (*pause*) I just kind of get the idea that you don't approve of this relationship I've started with this new woman I've met. (*pause*) It isn't anything you've said, particularly. I just kind of get that idea.
>
> **Therapist:** I think we learn a lot from your seeing me that way. You've mentioned a couple of times that your mother let you know how much she disapproved when you began to go out on dates. (*Client nods.*) I wonder if we're learning here that there was a good deal of buried anger in you back then. Perhaps that's why you're mad at me today and why you think I disapprove of your new relationship.

The genetic interpretation helps clients learn the extent to which they interpret contemporary reality in the light of their early experiences. To Gill, this discovery is the more powerful for having been made in the transference, where both parties can see it in its entirety.

Most classical psychoanalysts' transference interpretations were genetic. These interpretations have great value to Gill as well, for he believes as strongly as the classical analysts that clients need to learn the ancient origins of their contemporary functioning. But Gill cautions against overemphasizing genetic interpretations; we can become so immersed in our explorations of the past that we overlook work on the relationship with the therapist. If we make that mistake, we no longer have a re-experiencing therapy.

As Gill became more and more enthusiastic about the intersubjective paradigm, his work evolved in an important way. Since intersubjectivist therapists must be skeptical about everything in the therapy situation (their own subjectivity is just as suspect as their clients'), they cannot assess with any certainty what aspect of a client's experience reveals the client's templates and repetitions. The classical analysts had no doubt that the client's response to the therapist was determined by those templates. If I strongly objected to something my analyst did, she had little compunction about assuring me that I was actually experiencing some old feelings about my parents or perhaps that I was defending myself against feeling too close to her. She did not entertain the possibility that perhaps she had really done something outrageous. I'm sure she justified this stance, not unreasonably, by reminding herself that whatever she might or might not be guilty of, I wasn't paying for the privilege of supervising her; I deserved every possible opportunity to learn about my unconscious fantasies. Gill became convinced that the intersubjectivist could not afford such certainty.

The therapy situation has now become paradoxical. On the one hand, it is being constructed afresh every moment by the interacting subjectivities. On the other hand, the client does indeed bring unconscious expectations and ancient attitudes into the situation, and the therapy must afford him or her the opportunity to reflect upon them. So the therapist is now in the position of respectfully asking the client, as a collaborator, to explore the possible transference meanings of a given response.

The Therapist's Contribution to the Client's Experience

One aspect of Gill's notion of transference recognition remains to be explored. We have seen that Gill views therapy as an interpersonal situation in which the therapist contributes real cues to the client's experience. Inevitably clients perceive these cues and make the most plausible interpretation of them that they can. Equally inevitably, their interpretations are significantly shaped by the transference; that is, by their longstanding needs and expectations.

Gill reminds us that we do clients a serious disservice if we forget that we are not, after all, flawlessly programmed computers; we are imperfect humans, and we give off an assortment of signals of which we can at best be only partly aware.[20] Many of these cues stir in clients ideas about how we view them and how we feel about them. As we become increasingly important to them, these ideas attain ever-increasing significance.

When my clients accuse me of inconsistency, it is tempting to assume that they are merely expressing—at last—pent-up feelings about the inconsistencies of their parents. And, indeed, they often are. But it would be a costly error for me not to look also at the ways in which I have been inconsistent or at least the ways in which I must appear inconsistent to my clients.

Client: I think you're very inconsistent sometimes.

(The therapist ponders this idea a moment and realizes that she greeted the client less warmly today than she sometimes does.)

Therapist: I wonder if you thought I wasn't as warm to you as I usually am when you arrived today.

Client: That's right. Sometimes you like me and sometimes you don't. It would be easier for me if you liked me all the time.

(The therapist realizes that when the client arrived today, she had still been preoccupied by thoughts of the preceding client, but only for a few moments, and at least consciously she had felt perfectly friendly toward the present client when she'd settled down to work with him.)

Therapist: I think you're quite right that I wasn't as warm as usual when you arrived today. *(pause)* Your interpreting that as indicating I don't like you as much today seems altogether plausible. I can really see how you'd read it that way. *(pause)* I wonder, though, if you've considered that there are other interpretations. Perhaps I was distracted. So it might be of value to see why you chose that interpretation over some other ones that are equally plausible.

And the way is opened for exploring transference implications.

Validating the Client's Perception and Interpretation

The last scenario illustrates several of Gill's thoughts about this sort of interaction. First, he thinks it is important to validate the client's *perception*. This position is cleary at odds with that of the classical analyst, who is certain that everything the client thinks he sees in the therapist is mere transference and has nothing to do with anything the therapist actually did. In this case the validated perception is that the therapist was less warm than usual in her greeting today. Second, it is important for the therapist to affirm the plausibility of the client's interpretation. In this case the therapist labels as plausible the interpretation that she is not feeling very friendly toward the client today. Third, it is not necessary for the therapist to take a position on the truth of the client's interpretation. Gill believes that a therapist must never deny having the feeling that the client thinks he detects. Since the therapist is trying her best to teach the client the importance of the unconscious, she had better not deny that she may be influenced by something of which she is unaware. In fact, one should probably be cautious about ever adopting a posture of certainty.

Gill is less insistent that confession be avoided, but he is opposed to it. He thinks it seems to ask the client to withhold criticism ("I admit I did it; don't criticize me"). Also, confession deflects attention from the task—that of elucidating the client's feelings and expectations about the therapist. It is enough, Gill thinks, to validate the plausibility of the client's interpretation. We'll look at this issue more closely in Chapter 7.

Sometimes, Gill reminds us, clients have such a strong need to repeat old situations and they are so skilled at setting up a replay that they do succeed in getting the therapist to cooperate unwittingly with their transference wishes; that is, they manage to induce the therapist to behave in ways that satisfy their needs or fulfill their expectations. Despite my best intentions, if I am provoked skillfully enough, I may find myself flirtatious or irritable or uninterested. And, however subtly, I may act those feelings out.

Thus, there is another reason for us, as therapists, to pay close attention to what we ourselves do: by doing so we remain alert for and aware of our own countertherapeutic attitudes and behaviors, whether they come primarily from our own unconscious needs or have been induced to meet the client's unconscious needs. This is also an important reason for giving the client ample opportunity to tell us what he or she sees in us. The intersubjective paradigm has done away with the assumption that the client has nothing to teach us about how we may be colluding in acting out old patterns—the client's or ours. This topic will occupy us at length in Chapter 6.

The Therapeutic Relationship

We have seen Gill's two kinds of transference interpretation. The first, and the one to which he devotes the most attention, is aimed at helping clients become increasingly aware of their feelings about the therapist. The second is aimed at helping them see how their old attitudes determine their interpretation of the events of therapy. Gill offers us a valuable summary of his theory:

> If the therapist operates on the assumption that psychologically determined psychopathology is a matter of interpersonal relations; if he further believes that for purposes of the psychotherapy the most accurately demonstrable pattern of interpersonal interaction is that being enacted between the patient

and himself; and if he further believes that the explication of this pattern of interaction will result in the most far-reaching and stable beneficial influence on the patient's patterns of interaction, he will conclude that the elucidation of . . . the patient's experience of the relationship should be his primary goal. In pursuit of this goal he will be alert to disguised references by the patient to his experience of the relationship with the therapist in the here-and-now; he will make such references explicit, ever mindful that he may be mistaken; he will look first for the role which the patient is attributing to him in this experience, and he will attempt to make that explicit in a spirit of seeing the plausibility of the patient's experience even if that experience and the role attributed to him do not agree with what he subjectively considers to be his role.

Only after the patient's experience has been explored from this point of view will he raise questions about possible other interpretations of the ongoing interaction with the goal of elucidating the patient's transference contribution to his experience, . . . [that is, how the patient's experience of the relationship with the therapist] is significantly related to his past. But he will be ever mindful of a temptation on both his part and the patient's to flee to the exploration of the past from the probably more stressful examination of the present, and he will therefore be biased toward attention to the present rather than the past.[21]

Gill's premise is that remembering is not enough. Merely reconstructing the story of the client's life and the reasons for the client's difficulties is not by itself therapeutic. That exercise must be accompanied by an opportunity for the client to re-experience the old feelings and expectations in the presence of the new object of those feelings— that is, the therapist. If this re-experiencing is to be of value, the therapist must support and encourage it. In the past, these impulses met with a variety of self-serving responses. The therapist's nondefensive support and encouragement will be a unique experience for the client, and it is this experience that Gill sees as essential.

The therapist provides the opportunity for re-experiencing by assigning the highest priority to working with the transference. Gill is certainly not opposed to helping clients analyze events in their contemporary lives. He would not, for example, criticize a therapist for helping a client deepen her understanding of her relationships at home or at work. Nor is he opposed to helping a client understand the effect of his childhood experiences on his occupational or familial relationships. He thinks such help has a place in well-conducted therapy. But he believes the therapist brings about the most effective therapeutic change by working within the transference: that is, by continually increasing the client's awareness of the relationship.

The reasons are clear. First, Gill believes that it is in the clinical relationship that therapeutic re-experiencing is possible; therefore, that is where the greatest therapeutic leverage is to be found. Second, he believes that talk about other relationships and about childhood events, while certainly helpful, puts both therapist and client in danger of being seduced into intellectual formulations that may become more fascinating than useful. Thus Gill works as much as possible on encouraging the client to discuss the relationship with the therapist and, when necessary, on interpreting resistance to doing so.

To Gill, there is no possibility that the therapeutic situation can be neutral or the therapist a blank screen. Attempts to manipulate the situation to make it neutral may succeed only in presenting the client with a cold and unresponsive therapist. Gill encourages therapists to realize that therapy is inevitably an interpersonal situation and thus to permit themselves a good deal of spontaneity. To be spontaneous they must remain aware of the cues they give so that they may understand the client's responses.

Gill reminds therapists that this is an *intersubjective* situation. Both therapist and client view the events of the therapy through the lenses of their own templates and repetitions, their own unconscious fantasies. Each interprets and attempts to resolve the inevitable ambiguities through a unique lens. Gill reminds therapists that, just as the client is continually in the grip of transference, so they are continually in the grip of countertransference. Thus they may want to be somewhat skeptical about their own interpretations of events and willing to consider their clients' interpretations.

Finally, Gill believes that an effective therapist must demonstrate the utmost respect for the client, a genuine interest in the client's experience of the relationship, and an unflagging nondefensiveness in response to that experience. To the extent that the therapist manages to demonstrate those qualities, the situation becomes one that the client has never experienced before. And to the extent that the clinical relationship becomes unique in those ways, Gill teaches, it becomes truly therapeutic.

(5)

The Meeting of Psychoanalysis and Humanism

HEINZ KOHUT

Heinz Kohut (1913–1981) was an eminent member of the Freudian establishment; in fact, at one time he was president of the prestigious American Psychoanalytic Association. His training and credentials were impeccable. And yet his work has been the subject of one of the most acrimonious, energetic, and fruitful controversies in the history of psychoanalysis. There are those who see him as a destructive heretic and those who see him as the messiah. His critics fear that his growing popularity will undermine the foundations of psychoanalysis. They argue that for decades psychoanalysis has been fighting a lonely battle against conservative morality, and here is a renegade from the very heart of their club going over to the foe and trying to reduce the importance of sex and aggression in psychoanalytic theory. And equally costly, they believe, is his softening of the diamond-hard discipline of psychoanalytic practice by introducing into it the fuzzy warmth of humanism. His most fervent admirers, for their part, believe that his revolt was long overdue.

I see Kohut as neither heretic nor messiah, but rather as an uncommonly original psychoanalyst who significantly expanded our thinking about human development, psychopathology, and therapy, without taking anything away from the great insights of classical psychoanalytic theory. This is indeed Kohut's position: "It does not indicate any lack of respect for the great explanatory power of the classical formulations, or any lack of appreciation for their beauty and elegance, when I affirm now that it is possible, from the viewpoint of the psychology of the self . . . to enrich the classical theory by adding a self-psychological dimension."[1]

Kohut and Gill were both members of the Chicago Psychoanalytic Institute. Gill's first major work on his revolutionary transference theory appeared in 1982, the year after Kohut's death. Gill himself remained very much interested in Kohut's work, and wrote an in-depth study of the writings of Kohut and his associates.[2]

Like Gill, Kohut believed in the importance of the relationship between client and therapist and in the centrality of the transference. But Kohut offers us valuable ideas not found in Gill's work: he has proposed a theory of therapy based on a major and provocative revision of the psychoanalytic theory of development, he has identified forms of transference not previously recognized, he has given us a new understanding and appreciation of the value of empathy communicated to the client, and he has done more than anyone else to bring psychoanalysis and humanism together.

The Beginnings

Kohut traced the beginning of his movement away from standard psychoanalytic technique to an impasse he once reached with a female patient. In every session she hurled anguished, bitter accusations at him. He interpreted this hostility as resistance to his interpretations:

> I was inclined to argue with the patient about the correctness of my interpretations and to suspect the presence of stubborn hidden resistances. . . . For a long time I insisted . . . that the patient's reproaches related to specific transference fantasies and wishes on the Oedipal level. . . . She became [even more] violently angry, and furiously accused me of undermining her . . . and . . . wrecking her analysis.[3]

Kohut was convinced that he was dealing with a straightforward Oedipal transference and that his client was experiencing strong alternating feelings of love and hate for him. After getting nowhere with that approach, he finally stopped arguing with her and started listening. He began to realize that these urgent, persistent demands and accusations were not instances of resistance at all, but rather represented her attempt to show him the reality of her childhood.

The transference had reawakened some of her earliest memories. She had had a depressed and incapacitated mother who had been chronically unavailable to her. She was showing Kohut what that experience was like by making demands that no one had fulfilled in her early childhood. Looked at as the behavior of a grown person, the demands seemed so excessive and repetitive that they could easily be seen as resistance. But looked at as the demands of a young child trying her best to get her needs filled by an unresponsive mother, they could be seen as appropriate and thus extremely important for a therapist to understand.

Kohut's Two Questions

For twenty years Kohut pondered two questions: (1) What was it exactly that patients such as the angry woman hadn't gotten from their parents, and (2) what could a therapist do about it? He applied these questions to each client he saw and to his students' and colleagues' clients. His answers to these questions led him to diverge significantly from classical psychoanalysis. One of these divergences was theoretical, the other technical. The theoretical issue need concern us only briefly; the issue of technique is crucial to our topic.

The Theoretical Issue

Freud taught that the newborn infant sees the world as undifferentiated from itself. The infant cannot tell that it is separate from the person who holds and feeds it; all of its psychic energy—that is, all desire and frustration— is directed at this undifferentiated self. Freud called this the stage of primary narcissism. Narcissus, as you may recall, was the handsome Greek youth who spent his time gazing lovingly at his own reflection in a pool. Thus the word *narcissism,* to indicate the focusing of energy on the self.

As the child matures and comes to realize there are other people out there, some portion of the available energy is directed at those people—first, of course, at the primary caretaker. Slowly, as the child grows, more and more of the finite amount of available psychic energy is directed at the outside world, and less and less at the self. In Freud's terms, the child grows from a state of narcissism to one of object-relatedness. The more complete this shift, the healthier the person. In the fully mature adult, a relatively small amount of energy is still concerned with self issues.

Kohut gradually came to question whether this was the most useful way to view maturation. He proposed instead that there were two parallel lines of development, rather than the single one postulated by Freud. One of these lines was the one Freud described: an increasingly differentiated and mature capacity for object relatedness. The other line was the development of the self, which goes on throughout the lifetime of the healthy individual.[4]

The developmental theory of self psychology

In Kohut's view, three strong needs must be fulfilled if the self is to develop fully: the need to be "mirrored," the need to idealize, and the need to be like others.[5]

The need to be mirrored

The first need to arise is what Kohut called the grandiose-exhibitionistic need. Children need to be shown by one or both parents that they are special, wonderful, and welcome, that it is a great pleasure to have them around. Kohut taught that children learn how their parents value them not through anything the parents specifically say or do but through the most subtle of cues: gesture, expression, tone of voice. And presumably the message can be conveyed in varying degrees. To the parental message of delight in the child Kohut gave the name *mirroring*. The child looks to the parent for the answer to "Mirror, mirror on the wall, who's the most wonderful of them all?" If, a reasonable percentage of the time, the mirror replies,

"You are, my wonderful child," the grandiose-exhibition-istic need is met.[6]

Now, no parent can possibly be the perfect mirror all the time, and, Kohut says, that's a good thing for the child. Inevitably the parent will sometimes fail to provide adequate mirroring. If that failure doesn't happen too often or too traumatically, it provides the child with an opportunity. Children who have been well mirrored many, many times can draw on the memory of those experiences and thus discover an ability to get along without the mirror—at least for a brief time, at least once in a while. And when that happens, they discover that at least for a brief time, at least once in a while, they can be their own mirror. Kohut called this a "transmuting internalization,"[7] by which he meant that children seize the opportunity of the failed mirror to take the mirroring function upon themselves and, as a result, change something basic in their *self.* His way of describing that change was to say that bit by bit the child adds *structures* to the developing self. By structures Kohut referred to the adaptive and satisfying functions of the self. Gradually, as the child grows and develops, these transmuting internalizations and the structures they create add up to one important aspect of a strong and cohesive self. Now the grandiose-exhibition-istic needs are no longer primitive. Children who have been well mirrored no longer ask or care if they are the most wonderful one of all. They know that they are attractive and likable people, no matter what messages they may get from the outside world. Their self-esteem is firmly rooted, presumably forever.

If the parents are too disturbed or too preoccupied with questions of their own self-esteem, however, the child never gets enough of those early positive messages. The grandiose-exhibitionistic needs are traumatically frustrated and then repressed because it is too painful to be in touch with them when the child has no hope that they will ever be gratified.

Psychoanalytic theory teaches that one of the costs of repressing an important need is that the need does not become integrated into the developing personality. The need is walled off from the ego, and because the ego is the part of the personality that orchestrates integration and appropriate maturation, the need remains in its primitive form. This is the fate of grandiose-exhibitionistic needs that are not gratified. The person, then, is likely to suffer from insecurity and feelings of worthlessness, interrupted on occasion by surges of unrealistic grandiosity and, in some cases, maladaptive boasting when these powerful needs for mirroring burst momentarily through the barrier of repression and futilely strive for some crumbs of gratification. Thus a necessary structure of the self is stunted.[8]

The need to idealize

A second strong need of the developing self is the need for what Kohut called an *idealized parental imago*. It is important that the child can believe that at least one parent is powerful, calm, and confident. If this need is fulfilled, the child can count on help from that powerful, knowledgeable, and calm person in the face of an external world too complex for a youngster to comprehend and internal events too chaotic and frightening for an immature ego to deal with.[9]

Here, too, parents must sometimes fail. No parent is omnipotent or omniscient, and from time to time that fact will reveal itself even to a young child. And the child who has had repeated opportunities to identify with power and knowledge will be able to discover, when the failures come, some power and knowledge of her own. Thus, bit by bit, through the process of transmuting internalization, the child will come to see herself as powerful and to feel confident of her ability to cope both with the external world and with inevitable internal conflicts and pressures. This confidence is a key part of the self.

As this part of the self grows and matures through childhood into adolescence and beyond, it develops indispensable capacities. First, it is the repository of the *ideals* by which life is guided. Second, it exercises control over the impulses, enabling one to use them rather than to be overrun by them. Third, it develops the capacity for self-soothing in times of stress and pain.

We might pause here and note that all therapists know the importance of the capacity to soothe oneself. Many clients, perhaps most, lack this ability to a significant degree. Painful events happen to everyone. Everyone sometimes experiences anxiety and almost everyone sometimes experiences guilt or shame. The question is how a person responds to these experiences. According to Kohut, people who have successfully internalized a calm, powerful parental figure will expeditiously and quietly soothe themselves, deal with the situation, and go on. Many of our clients (and many of us), however, suffer prolonged, sometimes very prolonged, discomfort.

Finally, Kohut believed, the "higher" aspects of the personality—humor, empathy, creativity, and wisdom—come from a successfully internalized experience of an idealized parental imago.

Here the danger is that the child cannot idealize either parent. Perhaps the parents are locked into a pattern of denigrating each other before the child, or they may have such serious behavior problems that it is painfully obvious to the child that they simply are not candidates for idealization. The child will then have no opportunity to develop this part of the self. Kohut taught that when we meet people who seem to take no joy in life, to have no capacity to be inspired and little vitality, we may be seeing evidence that a need for an idealized parental imago was not met.

The need to be like others

The third need of the developing self Kohut called the *twinship* or *alter ego* need. He thought that children need to know that they share important characteristics with one or both of their parents, that they are not too different from the world into which they have been born. If this need is met, the growing person develops a sense of belonging, of communal status. If this need is not adequately met, children are in danger of feeling that in some basic way they are not like other people, that they are somehow strange and don't fit in.[10]

For much of his career, Kohut had thought that the self could most usefully be understood as having only two components—the grandiose-exhibitionistic and the idealized parental imago. He added the twinship need late in his career and consequently wrote less about it. For our purposes, it is enough to note that it's part of the self. It will be helpful to us in our effort to understand certain transferences.

The self

If these three needs are adequately met, the child develops a healthy self, which entails high self-esteem, a guidance system of ideals and values, and the self-confidence to develop one's competence. If these needs are not adequately met, the self will have deficits that interfere with healthy development and produce life problems of greater or lesser severity. Kohut called these problems self disorders. (It is interesting to note that he believed that if the parents successfully meet the child's needs in just one of the three areas—mirroring, idealizing, or alter ego—the child will not develop a serious self disorder, but will build what Kohut called *compensatory structures* in the area of the need that was successfully met.)[11] In fact, he came to believe that most us get along on compensatory structures. He thought that situation was not ideal, but that it was a good deal better than having had none of one's needs met.

I am a case in point: my mother suffered a severe and prolonged depression after my birth. I infer that I didn't get very much mirroring. I believe what I did to compensate was to lean heavily on my somewhat flimsy and very brief relationship with my father, whom I saw as physically and intellectually powerful. Kohut would perhaps say that in the idealizing aspect of my self I developed structures that compensated to some extent for the mirroring deficits.

When Kohut began to write about the psychology of the self, he believed he had found a new way of understanding a single diagnostic group, the disorders that had been called narcissistic: he thought these problems arose from an incompletely developed self, and they were the ones he referred to when he spoke of self disorders. But by the end of his life he and his co-workers had become convinced that there are few of us who don't have self problems of greater or lesser severity, and even fewer among people who seek a therapist's help.[12]

Kohut called his theory of development *self psychology,* defining the self as the part of the personality that is cohesive in space, enduring in time, the center of initiative, and the recipient of impressions. This self is made up of the structures that result from the transmuting internalizations.[13]

Kohut taught that the development and maturation of the self is a lifelong process, and that throughout life a person experiences recurring needs for people (Kohut called them selfobjects) who will furnish mirroring experiences, serve as idealized imagoes, and satisfy alter ego needs for belonging. Kohut's theory is a useful counterweight to the quite common belief that as mature adults we are supposed to do it all on our own, that only the weak *need* other people. Kohut called this the false "maturity morality" of our culture and of classical psychoanalysis, and repeatedly reminded us that there is nothing immature in the lifelong need for selfobjects. Gill is one of many psychoanalysts who have expressed their gratitude to Kohut for this emphasis.

The relation of self psychology to Freud's theory of development

That, in greatly simplified form, is Kohut's theory of development. Before we move on to consider his clinical theory, we should consider for a moment the relation of Kohut's self psychology to Freud's theories of psychosexual development and psychopathology. An exploration of those theories is beyond the scope of this book, but since we are working toward an integration of Kohut, Rogers, and Gill, and since Gill's theories of development and psychopathology draw so heavily on Freud, we should ask whether Kohut's conception of the self's development is supplementary to Freud's or opposed to it.

It is widely held these days that all the object relations theories, including Kohut's, are irreconcilably opposed to Freud's theories of motivation, development, and psychopathology.[14] Till the last years of his life, Kohut rejected that view; he held that he was building on classical psychoanalytic theory, not competing with it. The theory of self development was not a replacement for the theory of psychosexual development; it was an addition to it.

I think it is helpful to view Freud's theories as illuminating the effects of one's intrapsychic history and those of Kohut and other object relations theorists as showing us the effects of one's interpersonal history. Each view makes a unique contribution to our understanding of the client, and each contributes to our understanding of how the client views the therapist. Replaying the Oedipal drama, a client may see the therapist as an object of desire or fear. Or, revealing an unsatisfied wish for an idealized parental imago, the client might see the therapist as the perfect parent. An alert therapist will be prepared to recognize either.

It thus seems to me that the theories are compatible, and that therefore we can integrate Gill's and Kohut's views of the clinical relationship. I trust that integration will become clear as we proceed.

We noted earlier that Kohut was concerned with two questions: What exactly was it that his client hadn't gotten from her parents, and what could a therapist do about it? We have had a glimpse of his answer to the first question. Now let's concern ourselves with the second.

The Issue of Therapeutic Technique

If Gill is our spokesperson for a less stony and formal aura within the psychoanalytic tradition, Kohut, within that same tradition, went a long step further. We will see in a moment that it is quite unfair to accuse him of being nothing but a kindly handholder, although kindness is certainly an important part of his therapy. It has been repeatedly observed that Kohut represents a coming together of the humanistic and psychoanalytic traditions, and one major reason for this observation is his insistence that therapists express their humanity.

A corrective emotional experience?

In the mid-1940s the psychoanalyst Franz Alexander described successful therapy as a *corrective emotional experience*.[15] Alexander believed that clients had gotten into trouble and sought therapy because the people who raised them had not treated them well. What they needed was someone significant to treat them better, and Alexander proposed to be that someone. For reasons that are not altogether clear, at least not to me, the concept of the corrective emotional experience has received very bad press over the years. Perhaps therapists saw it as implying reassurance at the expense of learning. Perhaps it evoked images of kindly volunteers giving patients milk and cookies. One can understand how therapists may have felt diminished by this image and feared that it didn't give enough weight to the cognitive aspects of their work. After all, they were engaged in deciphering a complex code—that of the unconscious—and helping patients learn through analysis. What's more, many of them, as we have seen, have always prided themselves on being intellectually and emotionally tough. They were certainly not dispensing milk and cookies.

A related objection may have come from the implication that the corrective emotional experience was to be *gratifying*. We have seen that many therapists argue against gratifying a client's needs on the ground that gratification only prolongs the problem by keeping the client from learning what a hard world this is. Thus they object to an intentionally warm and supportive experience. The dogged avoidance of providing such an experience presents the client with a frustrating situation. Many schools of therapy acknowledge the inevitable frustration cheerfully and say it's all part of the design: no one gives up a familiar old position without being motivated by some frustration. Kohut took another tack and argued that a nonempathic therapist is pouring gasoline on the fire. The client got into trouble by being raised in this kind of environment, and more of the same isn't going to help much. As we'll see, however, Kohut acknowledged the need for a certain *kind* of frustration.

With the advantage of hindsight, objections to the idea of therapy as a corrective emotional experience seem pretty silly. Ever since Freud discovered that it was not enough merely to tell patients the reasons for their trouble, therapists have been providing one or another sort of corrective emotional experience. Nonetheless, objections still are raised.

Empathy

And so, wryly accepting that he was courting his colleagues' disapproval, Kohut said that it is indeed the task of the therapist to provide a corrective emotional experience, and that the main component of that experience is *empathy*.[16] In Kohut's view, therapeutic empathy has nothing in common with milk and cookies: "The best definition of empathy . . . is that it is the capacity to think and feel oneself into the inner life of another person. It is our lifelong ability to experience what another person experiences, though usually . . . to an attenuated degree."[17] To Kohut the first job of all therapists is to open themselves to the empathic experience that permits them to see the world from the client's point of view. The next task is to let the client know that the therapist has indeed succeeded in seeing the situation from the client's perspective. Probably no therapist would deny the importance of empathizing with the client. Kohut differs from many other therapists in the emphasis he puts on *letting clients know that you're doing your best to understand the way things look to them.*

An occupational hazard: Being critical

One major implication of this position is that therapists don't tell clients that their view is wrong. Kohut observed that many therapists tend to be critical of their clients. One can understand why. Therapists are only human and thus are prey to the whole range of human foibles, including impatience, unconscious aggressiveness, self-protectiveness, sadistic impulses, and power urges. In other words, therapists are subject to all the vagaries of countertransference.

Besides those inevitable dangers, many therapists hold theoretical beliefs that can easily slip over into justifications of criticism:

The belief that clients make life harder than necessary. When Freud first described resistance and defense, they were seen as unconscious mechanisms that protected the person against what seemed to be real dangers. But years of thinking of clients as people who ask for help and then do everything possible to interfere with the helper's efforts can easily lead a therapist into behaving as though clients were bad children who were purposely making life hard for the therapist.

The belief that self-reliance and self-responsibility are necessary for growth. Kohut believed that the culture at large and the psychotherapy community in particular had developed the puritanical view that the only real adults were those who were so strong and self-reliant that, though they enjoyed and appreciated other people, they could get along just as well on their own. Therapists can readily slip into a critical stance when they confront what they perceive to be a client's dependency. This attitude starts with perfect goodwill: I really want my clients to achieve independence and self-reliance because I fear that excessive dependency puts them at the mercy of other people's whims. This wish produces subtle exhortations, and before I know it I am being openly critical. I have gotten caught up in the value system that says independence statements are good and should be rewarded, while dependency statements are bad and should be "confronted." Now I am just the latest version of the clients' parents and teachers and preachers, telling them they're doing it wrong.

A corollary to this belief in independence is the distaste many therapists feel for statements that portray the client as a victim. Even if we all agree that clients will be better off when they stop seeing themselves this way (and I certainly feel that way about most clients and about myself), Kohut was most emphatic in his insistence that criticizing such statements only confirms clients' belief in their victimization—now by the critical therapist.

The belief that immature behaviors should not be encouraged. Some of this belief springs from countertransference: therapists are often offended by a client's primitive expressions of narcissism, such as unmodulated boasting or unmasked fishing for approval. And some of it springs from a theoretical position that holds that the therapist's job is to show the client how immature these behaviors are. According to Kohut, it is not helpful to view these expressions as childish reluctance to give up old gratifications.

He asked therapists to see them as welcome indications that clients have not abandoned the hope of having their narcissistic needs met. At a deep level, clients understand the necessity for fully expressing these needs in order to complete the healthy development of the self and go on to more mature gratifications. These immature expressions are signs that the organism has not been killed, that life energy remains and growth is still possible.

The belief that transference is distortion. It is dangerously easy to sound critical when we inform clients that they don't see us the way we really are. Both Gill and Kohut continually remind us that this is a particularly costly form of criticism, since we are trying our best to help clients feel free to talk about their feelings for us. That is hard enough for clients to do under the best of circumstances; they need all the support they can get.

There is nothing wrong with those views, at least in moderation. Independence certainly has value. Defense and resistance are to be expected and have to be contended with. There is nothing wrong with these beliefs; the problem is the critical and judgmental mind-set into which they seduce us. We want clients to reveal themselves to us. If we are empathic, they will gradually come to trust us. If we punish their revelations, we will teach them to suppress any thoughts they have learned will be criticized.

Kohut taught that lack of empathic acceptance by parents drives whole segments of the personality underground. There they retain their archaic form and are split off from the modulating and maturing influence of the ego. The therapist is not going to help by repeating the process. Instead, Kohut counseled, it is necessary to create conditions in which these buried aspects of the self can emerge into the light and be empathically accepted. As these aspects reach consciousness, the process of integrating them into the adult personality can begin.

Thus Kohut shared Gill's concern that we not tell clients that their experience is wrong. Empathy means letting clients know that, perhaps for the first time, they are truly understood. And it further means letting them know that, also perhaps for the first time, the way they see the world is accepted as a plausible way for them to see it, given their individual histories.

When a client is resisting, a therapist may respond in either of two ways. The first is to see resistance as an obstacle to be somehow gotten around or through. The classically trained therapist is likely to interpret the resistance: "Perhaps you are avoiding some uncomfortable feelings." Kohut looked at resistance as an adaptive protection of the threatened self, and empathized with it as he did with everything a client might say, trying his best to see the resistance from the client's perspective. Thus his empathy encompassed the resistance and the feelings that were threatening the client.

Imagine a client who tends to chatter. After a time Kohut might say, "You know, I can imagine that there are things that seem scary to talk about in here. So it makes sense to me that you'd want to stick to safe topics while you build your trust in me."

Does the therapist actually provide the mirror?

Those who accuse Kohut of serving milk and cookies read him as saying that the therapist's job is to correct the deficit in a client who was never adequately mirrored by actually doing the mirroring in therapy; that is, by repeatedly telling clients that they are indeed the fairest ones of all—or at least that they're pretty fair. That's a seriously incorrect reading. Kohut thought that such behavior would be countertherapeutic. What he thought is therapeutic is to learn carefully how problems stem from the client's childhood, repeatedly communicating that the client's way of being is understandable and understood. (Kohut reminded us never to derogate the client's parents, rather bearing in mind that those parents themselves had parents.) So instead of saying that the client is the fairest, Kohut might say that the client's feelings of worthlessness were altogether understandable in view of the lack of positive response she received as a child. Arnold Goldberg, one of Kohut's closest associates, puts it this way:

> Analysts gratify neither the demands for mirroring archaic grandiosities nor the demands for approval from archaic idealized self-objects. These demands [are] consistently interpreted . . . in a tactful, nonhurtful, nonhumiliating manner. . . . The analyst does not actively mirror; he interprets the need for confirming responses. The analyst does not actively admire or approve grandiose expectations; he explains their role in the psychic economy.[18]

There is something intuitively powerful about this distinction. If my therapist tells me I'm wonderful, I'm glad he thinks so, but I have to wonder if this is nothing but therapeutic technique, if he says the same thing to everyone, and if it really says anything at all about my worth. And even if I were to believe he thinks so, that's not the same thing as my thinking so. When I was a child, my parents were essentially my only source of information about the world, and I was a blank slate on which any message might be written. Those conditions no longer exist, and as we all know to our cost, our self-image is likely to be improved only temporarily by having a loved one tell us we're wonderful.

If, however, my therapist really understands what it is like to be me and helps me see that I am like this not because of some inherent badness but because of the inevitable laws of cause and effect, a different attitude toward myself becomes possible, and with it comes the possibility of change.

Kohut put it this way: A crucially important task for an adult is to be able to seek out people (selfobjects) who will gratify one's mature narcissistic needs. (You may recall that to Kohut *narcissistic* is not a derogatory term. Narcissistic energy is a valuable and important part of one's personality.) Once one has found these selfobjects, it is important to be able to accept the mature narcissistic gratifications they offer—through mirroring, through being idealized, or through serving as an alter ego. Those of us who have self disorders, and I think there must be a lot of us, perpetuate our difficulty (1) by not seeking out people who can offer these gratifications, (2) by seeking primitive forms of these gratifications, or (3) by being unable to accept mature gratifications when they are offered. To Kohut, one goal of therapy is to help clients become more and more able to get these needs met.[19] Therapists who meet those needs themselves, Kohut taught, do not increase their clients' ability to find selfobjects on their own.

What sort of frustration is helpful?

We observed that many schools of therapy teach that some kind of frustration is necessary to motivate clients to move from the familiar to the new, particularly to the frighteningly new. And we saw that Kohut did not disagree with that reasoning, though he had no high opinion of the kind of frustration that comes from therapeutic coldness or nonempathic responses. Optimal therapeutic frustration, he thought, comes from a different source. At the most primitive level, clients want to be gratified *as children*; that is, they want to be hugged, to be told that they're wonderful, that you will protect them, and so forth. For all the empathy he provided, Kohut did not provide these gratifications. In the context of a warm, supportive empathy, this is the optimal frustration, which motivates change and growth.

Let's look at the difference between actually doing the mirroring and empathically communicating to the client that you have grasped the intensity of the need for that mirroring.

Client: The people at work don't seem to find me very interesting. I'm beginning to see that no one really wants to spend much time with me or go out to lunch with me or anything like that. The truth of the matter is that I don't think I'm a very interesting person or very attractive, for that matter. (*stops and looks expectantly at the therapist*)

Some therapists are tempted to say at that point, "Well, I find you interesting, and I think you're quite attractive." It's particularly tempting to say this sort of thing if it's true. So that's one alternative. Another (the classic psychoanalytic) is to remain silent and wait. Kohut advised neither. In order to understand what he recommended, we must keep in mind his conviction that the manner is as important as the words. What follows must be said with warmth and compassion, or else it will be heard as criticism. And Kohut's first priority was not to be heard as critical.

Therapist: (*trying his best to feel inside himself what it would be like to have such experiences*) It must be extremely painful to believe that people don't find you interesting or attractive.

Client: (*still expectantly*) It really is.

(*It's now inescapably clear that what is wanted is reassurance.*)

Therapist: I would think that with that much insecurity about your being attractive and interesting to people, you must have an overwhelming need to know if that's really true and if people do respond to you that way. I think you must often have that need here—to know if I find you interesting and attractive.

Client: It's true. I think about that stuff all the time.

Therapist: That must be very painful.

(*Suppose the client isn't willing to let it go at that.*)

Client: Well, how about it? Isn't it true that you feel all those things about me, too?

Therapist: I really understand what a major issue this is for you. And I think I can be much more useful to you by helping you learn about this subject than I could by just being one more person with an opinion about you. My opinions are no better than anyone else's. I think my value to you lies somewhere else. This is a hugely important subject for you. We'll do a lot better trying

                to understand it than we will settling for
                some momentary reassurance.

Client: It is a big subject. I guess it's the biggest.

Kohut's psychoanalytic critics might cry foul here and say that the therapist who works this way has actually answered the question, if not in words, then in manner. By his warmth, his interest, and his concern he has said a good deal about the client's worth. And I think Kohut would have replied: "Guilty as charged." Warmth and interest are indeed parts of the corrective emotional experience that Kohut thought therapy must be. And he would have added that this warm and empathic understanding of the hard path the client has walked is utterly different from pronouncing the client the fairest one of all.

Understanding and explanation

Kohut saw therapy as consisting of two elements: understanding and explanation.[20]

Understanding. Therapists' first job is to understand their clients, as deeply and completely as possible. The tool for this understanding is empathy, and the prerequisite is extreme openness. Kohut taught that therapists must be willing to let go of their preconceptions and their theories as they turn their capacity for empathy to the client. The task is not to figure out where the client fits into one's theory; the task is to understand the client's experience as fully as possible. "If there is one lesson that I have learned during my life as an analyst," Kohut wrote, "it is the lesson that what my patients tell me is likely to be true—that many times when I believed that I was right and my patients were wrong, it turned out, though only after a prolonged search, that my rightness was superficial whereas their rightness was profound."[21] We have seen how Gill's refusal to view transference phenomena as distortions leads to considerable respect for the client. Kohut's strong conviction that clients are the experts on themselves deepens that respect.

Here again Kohut's approach brings humanistic psychology and the psychoanalytic tradition together. Humanistic therapists and group leaders, led by Carl Rogers, have long insisted that clients are the experts on themselves. Traditionally this stance has been seen as the direct opposite of the psychoanalytic position, with its notions of the unconscious, resistance, and defense, all of which imply that clients know little about themselves. And now here is a psychoanalyst teaching that clients know what they need a good deal better than the therapist, and that the therapist would do well to listen carefully and attempt to grasp the client's experience empathically. Robert Stolorow once said that Kohut seemed to be working his way to an intersubjectivist position, and if he had lived longer he would eventually have reached it. Kohut's reluctance to believe that his perspective was any more correct than the patient's is a significant case in point.

The first task is to understand and convey one's understanding to the client. Like Rogers before him, Kohut believed that this experience in itself is therapeutic. If you do nothing but strive for the deepest possible understanding of the client, and if you communicate that understanding, that experience could be life changing for the client. That proposition seems intuitively correct, doesn't it? Certainly it would be unique in my experience to be with someone whose first priority was to understand the finest details of my experience and to let me know that they had indeed been grasped. This is what Rogers called feeling prized. It's hard to believe that it wouldn't have a profound effect on my view of myself.

Recently I had to close my office and see clients temporarily in another place. One of my clients refused to meet me there because the parking situation was too difficult. She was angry and contemptuous that I would even ask her to go there. I committed a whole list of Kohut sins. I told her that parking was no harder there than anywhere else and that I assumed there was something else underlying her anger. She got angrier and angrier, and finally I did, too. The confrontation escalated into a near disaster. Kohut would have felt his way into her situation and said with warmth and understanding, "I can really see how upsetting it is for you to have the stability of our seeing each other disturbed. I think that figuring out where you'd park really is difficult, and I think there must be a lot of other upsetting things about our having to see each other somewhere else. And I can imagine some of those other things are even harder to talk about than the parking problem." Had she then kept the fight going, he might have said, "I think it must be really hard to have this move just laid on you—to have no say in the matter. It must seem like just one more instance when you get pushed around, when decisions get made for you, when you have to take it or leave it. It must be very hard."

Had I done that, I might have made it possible for her to explore other feelings—or I might have failed to do so. But whatever the outcome, she would have felt heard and understood. As it was, I became just one more in a long series of people telling her she was doing it wrong.

Explanation. Understanding, in Kohut's view, is therapeutic as far as it goes, but complete therapy also requires *explanation*—helping clients see that what they do or what they feel or how they are relating to the therapist makes perfect sense, given their life history.

In the situation with my angry client, if the therapy were far enough along so that I had the information, and if I thought the client was ready for it, Kohut might have wanted me to go on to say, "It's very understandable that you've had such a strong response to this change. We know how inconsistent and undependable your father was. You could never count on him for anything. So it makes perfect sense that you'd be badly upset by any inconsistency or unreliability in our relationship."

Explanation has three functions:

1. It helps clients see the roots of their behaviors and increases their cognitive understanding of themselves.

2. Kohut, like Gill, was a re-experiencing therapist, and we might expect him to see *relationship* value in the explanation process. Indeed he did. Explanation deepens the sense of being understood. If my therapist understands how these behaviors came to be, if she understands that I'm in trouble not because of some inherent badness but because of my early experiences, then she really does understand me. Understands and accepts me.

3. And to Kohut, who was a relationship therapist, explanation had still another value: therapist and client become colleagues building an explanatory system; their relationship is at a level of greater complexity and maturity than one based merely on empathy. Thus the client learns to relate to the therapist and to others on a more mature level.

Together, understanding and explanation have many therapeutic values: they create a climate of growth, they increase clients' understanding of their lives, and they put more and more of clients' behaviors under ego control. In addition, they enable clients to build new self-structures.

Transmuting internalizations in therapy

You will recall that in Kohut's theory of development, the structures that make up the self are slowly built through *transmuting internalizations*.[22] When parents are for the most part supportive, as mirrors, idealized imagoes, and alter egos, their occasional failures give children a chance to provide those functions for themselves. Our clients have gotten into trouble because their parents failed them in some or all of those functions. So the therapeutic task is to give clients a chance to build the structures that didn't get built when the clients were children. In Kohut's view, self structures are built in therapy just as they are in childhood. If the therapist is *mostly* empathic, the conditions are set for structure building. Just as it is impossible for a parent to be perfectly understanding, perfectly empathic all the time, so it is impossible for a therapist to be perfect. Failures are inevitable. The therapist may be in a bad mood or distracted or just miss what the client is saying. And besides, no therapist can be available all the time. Everyone gets sick. Everyone takes vacations. No one is always there to answer the phone. If these failures don't come too often and aren't too traumatic, and if the therapist acknowledges a failure with empathy and without defensiveness, the opportunity presented by the inevitable failures of a good parent now presents itself again. The client discovers an ability to provide some of that nourishing empathy unassisted. Each such experience is a transmuting internalization, and a bit of structure is added to the self. In successful therapy, the structures are built slowly over time, until the original deficits are healed or until adequate compensatory structures have been built. As in Gill's model, nondefensiveness on the part of the therapist is the key to success.

Let's look at how this process might work:

Client:	I'm really not looking forward to coming here these days.
	(*Just as in Gill's model—as in any inter-subjectivist model— the therapist silently reviews recent events to see if this reaction could have been prompted by something the therapist said or did. Kohut's first thought would be: "Have I been guilty of a failure of empathy?" A classically trained thera-pist, in contrast, would be likely to wonder first what material had recently surfaced that was causing the client anxiety.*)
Therapist:	Can you say more about that?
Client:	Not really. I used to look forward to being here, but lately I'm really not look-ing forward to coming in.
Therapist:	It occurs to me that a couple of weeks ago I told you the dates of my summer vacation. I wonder if I wasn't sensitive enough to how that news would affect you.
Client:	Well, I think it's true that I've been thinking that there isn't much sense in getting too deeply into anything as long as you're not going to be here.
Therapist:	That makes a lot of sense to me. I remember that when you were living with

> your grandmother, she used to go away
> without telling you when she'd be back. I
> remember how distressing that was for
> you. So it's really understandable that you
> would be upset about my vacation, par-
> ticularly since I was somewhat cavalier in
> the way I told you about it.

It is always tempting to blame the client for one's own failure of empathy. In the incident with my angry client, my first response was to feel self-righteous and silently blame her for being so outraged about the parking problem, which seemed pretty silly to me. Such defensiveness is always tempting—and it is very costly. In Kohut's model the main advantage of nondefensiveness is that it helps clients to realize that the failure is not theirs; that realiza- tion in turn enables them to provide the missing empathy for themselves and thus begin the process of repairing the self.

As we recall Gill's distinction between the remembering and re-experiencing schools of therapy, it seems clear that Kohut, like Gill, was firmly on the side of re-experiencing.

Forms of transference

You will recall Freud's observation that the client's view of the therapist is forced into shapes determined by the client's earliest relationships (the client's templates) and is further influenced by the human tendency to repeat certain old patterns (the repetition compulsion). Kohut added another hugely important observation: Once clients discover that they have found someone who is willing to listen to them empathically, the old unmet needs awaken and they look upon the therapist as a self- object. They may see the therapist as someone who can at last meet the old hunger to be mirrored, as someone whom they can at last idealize and from whom they can draw strength, or as someone like them in some important way, someone whose presence enables them to feel like full members of the human race. Kohut called these experiences "selfobject transferences." He identified three such transferences, and he thought it likely that others would be identified someday: the *mirror transference,* the *idealizing transference,* and the *twinship transference.*[23]

The discovery of the selfobject transferences is one of Kohut's major contributions to the understanding of psychotherapy. Therapists are now in a position to assess whether a transference phenomenon is a repetition of old expectations or a hope for something new and healing, and they can respond accordingly. Stolorow and his associates have a valuable way of viewing the relationship between these two manifestations of transference. They describe a "bipolar conception of transference":

> At one pole of the transference is the patient's longing to experience the analyst as a source of requisite selfobject functions that were missing or insufficient during the formative years. In this dimension of the transference, the patient hopes and searches for a new selfobject experience that will enable him to resume and complete an arrested developmental process. At the other pole are the patient's expectations and fears of a transference repetition of the original experiences of selfobject failure. It is this second dimension of the transference that becomes the source of conflict and resistance.
>
> We believe that a well-conducted psychoanalysis is characterized by inevitable, continual shifts in the figure-ground relationships between the experiential foreground and background of the treatment. These oscillations correspond to shifts in the patient's psychological organization and motivational priorities that occur in response to alterations in the tie to the analyst—shifts and alterations that are profoundly influenced by whether or not the analyst's interpretive activ-

ity is experienced by the patient as being attuned to his affective states and needs. For example, when the analyst is experienced as unattuned, foreshadowing a traumatic repetition of early selfobject failure, the conflictual and resistive dimension of the transference is frequently brought into the foreground, while the patient's selfobject yearnings are, of necessity, driven into hiding. On the other hand, when the analyst is able to analyze accurately the patient's experience of selfobject failure, demonstrating his attunement to the patient's reactive affect states and thereby mending the ruptured tie, the selfobject pole of the transference becomes restored and strengthened and the conflictual/resistive/repetitive dimension tends to recede into the background.

It is our contention that the mode of the therapeutic action of psychoanalysis differs depending on whether it is the selfobject or the conflictual dimension of the transference that occupies the position of foreground at any particular juncture of the treatment.

When the conflictual dimension is preeminent in the transference, an essential ingredient of the working through process concerns the interpretive illumination of the patient's unconscious organizing activity as discerned within the intersubjective dialogue between patient and analyst. We refer here to the ways in which the patient's experience of the analyst and his activities—especially his interpretive activity—is unconsciously and recurrently patterned by the patient according to developmentally preformed meanings and invariant themes, usually taking the form of expectations and fears of retraumatization.[24]

When Kohut first developed the idea that certain problems arose from an incompletely developed self, he saw these problems as distinct diagnostic categories and made the diagnosis by observing the nature of the transference. He said you couldn't really tell whether you were dealing with a self disorder until you had begun the treatment and could see what sort of transference developed. In this early formulation, he thought that the therapy he was recommending was appropriate only for self disorders, which were diagnosed by the emergence of a selfobject transference, and that classical psychoanalysis was still the preferred treatment for the psychoneuroses.

My angry client with the parking problem, for instance, fitted Kohut's description of the person who "self-righteously demanded exclusive attention and reassuring praise—because her phase-appropriate needs for mirroring had not been met by her self-absorbed mother." Kohut considered this sort of behavior as indicative of a "mirror transference" (that is, the mirror form of a selfobject transference), and so would have diagnosed her as having a "mirror-hungry personality," a form of narcissistic personality disorder.[25]

A client who looked to the therapist to be someone who could be "admired for his prestige, power, beauty, intelligence, or moral stature" he saw as forming an "idealizing transference," which suggests the diagnosis of "ideal-hungry personality," another form of narcissistic personality disorder.[26]

These narcissistic personality disorders are the sort of self disorders for which he originally thought his therapeutic method was the treatment of choice.

As his work progressed and he began to think that most of us suffer from a self disorder to some degree, he talked less about the need to decide whether a client suffered from a self disorder or from some other kind of problem; he came increasingly to believe that his therapeutic principles were applicable to a much wider range of human disturbances than he had once thought.

Few contemporary therapists are likely to use transference content as the sole diagnostic tool. Nonetheless, I think Kohut's classifications of transference phenomena can be valuable as reminders of the things that might have gone wrong in the client's development.[27]

Sometimes a client begins to tell me what a good therapist I am and how he brags to his friends about me. I used to assume automatically that the client was buttering me up to keep me from leading the therapy into dangerous territory, or perhaps was expressing a reaction formation against feelings of anger. Kohut taught me to consider the possibility that this is an idealizing transference and that it should be treated with interest and respect. It should also be treated as a strong indication that as a child this client may have had insufficient opportunity to idealize a parent. It indicates, too, that, however insufficiently, he has managed to idealize a parent to *some* degree. If he had had no experience of idealization at all, he would not even have enough hope to seek it in the transference. All of the selfobject transferences—the mirror transference, the idealizing transference, and the twinship transference—are extremely positive. They represent clients' hope; they show that they haven't stopped trying to get those needs met.

Let's look at some examples. A client spends time expressing in various ways the hope and the belief that he is the therapist's favorite client. The therapist identifies this as a mirror transference and resists all temptation to lead the client to more "mature and realistic" modes of function. The therapist says, in a warm and supportive manner, "It really is important to you that I like working more with you than with anyone else. And it certainly is understandable. We know how many kids there were in your family and how little time your mother had to pay any attention to you, even when you were very young. It's no wonder you have a strong need to know you're special."

Male client to male therapist: Sometimes it's nice just to hang out with you, without saying

too much. You're about my age, and
sometimes I think we could have been
good friends if we'd met some other way.
I like it that you smoke a pipe like I do.
It's nice just hanging out.

(*A classical analyst might see this as a resistance maneuver; "hanging out," after all,
is a good deal safer than talking about possibly dangerous material. The self psychologist doesn't focus on this possibility because
he recognizes the phenomenon as a twinship
transference. He lights his pipe and they
smoke quietly for a time.*)

Therapist: I get it. (*Then after a long pause*) I
remember how you never had much
chance to just hang out with your father,
how he was always too busy to have time
for you. (*Or, if it's earlier in the therapy
and this information hasn't yet appeared*)
Did you have much chance, as a kid, to
hang out with your father?

A couple of words are in order about twinship transferences. First of all, they are not confined to therapists and
clients of the same sex. Second, unlike the other transference types, they can be satisfied in silence. Kohut teaches
that a child needs to *hear* from the mirroring parent and
the idealized parent. But the twinship person, be it parent,
grandparent, or someone else, is different. The typical
activity that satisfies the need for the child is spending
time with the same-sex parent, quietly cooking, or doing
woodwork, or watching television. (It need not be the
same-sex parent, but that's the typical model.)

The importance of revealing one's humanity

We observed in Chapter 1 that the psychoanalytic and humanistic traditions were coming together in ways that presented new opportunities for therapists to combine the power of the psychodynamic theories with the equal power of a truly humane relationship. Kohut's work represents one of the most important forces in that movement. Though a psychoanalyst to the core, as well as a firm believer in the power of the unconscious and in the importance of analyzing the transference, he was unflagging in his efforts to free therapists from the rigid values of the past—values that have led to countertherapeutic coldness, judgmental behavior, and, perhaps most destructive of all, defensiveness.

He counseled therapists to permit themselves a relaxed and easy going manner and a good deal of emotional availability. In his final book he says, "I have come to feel freer, and, without guilt and misgivings, to show [my clients] my deep involvement and concern via the warmth of my voice, the words that I choose, and other similarly subtle means."[28]

The importance of nondefensiveness

Like Gill, Kohut reminded us that defensiveness is one of the therapist's most dangerous enemies. When we are under attack, he counseled, the first rule is not to fight back. Most of us are too sophisticated to get *caught* doing such a thing. So we fight back with interpretations and subtle accusations of defensiveness and resistance. Kohut thought this sort of response was a bad mistake: If we can empathize with clients, we can open ourselves to discovering just how they see us. Of course, their view may not coincide with the way we see ourselves, but we're not there

to empathize with ourselves; we're there to empathize
with our clients. And empathizing with clients when
they're seeing us in a bad light is very hard—and very
therapeutic. This is a good time to invoke the intersubjective insights and remember that our perspective may be no
more objective than the client's. Sometimes a client may
exaggerate some failure of the therapist's and blow up a
small error into a major one. It's tempting to criticize the
exaggeration, but it's not a good idea. In this situation
Kohut would have the therapist say something like this to
the client: "I can imagine how upsetting it must be for you
to believe that I've made such a serious error." Gill and
Kohut are aligned in assigning importance to nondefensiveness. To Gill it is what makes the re-experience different from the original experience. To Kohut it is the necessary precondition for empathy. To both it is indispensable.

The Liberated Therapist

The therapist who feels free to empathize with clients
affords them:

1. A sense of being listened to by someone truly willing
to work at understanding them.

2. A sense of having been deeply understood.

3. A sense of having been accepted, whether they are
experiencing and expressing a conflictual or a selfobject
transference.

4. An opportunity to learn the ancient roots of their difficulties through the therapist's explanations and thus
to make sense of those difficulties.

5. An opportunity to build new self structures, particularly new structures to compensate for old deficits. These structures are built through transmuting internalizations after the therapist has failed in empathy.

These are the major aspects of the therapist–client relationship that Kohut thought most helpful to clients.

I believe that Kohut has done a good deal more than produce a new theory of narcissism and a new technique of therapy. He offered us, I think, a new freedom to relate to our clients with a spirit of friendly and open generosity that many therapists have long felt as their natural way, but a way denied them by the looming conscience of their profession.

6

Countertransference

〜

A client I particularly like, who happens to be a graduate student in psychology, said to me one day, "On Rogers' eight-point empathy scale I'd give you about a three." I felt a rush of indignant hurt flash through my body. It lasted only a moment, and then I set to work suppressing it. This is wonderful, I said to myself. I've been waiting for the negative transference for months, and here it is.

Deep down, the hurt was still struggling to make itself known.

I'm the one supposed to be watching the store around here, I said to myself. My defenses won the struggle, the hurt was successfully suppressed, and with relief I reestablished my faith in the myth of psychotherapy: In this room there is one distressed person with problems and one professional who has it all together.

If you were to ask me if that is what I believe, I would assure you that I believe no such thing; I know only too well that I don't have it all together. Yet when I'm in the consulting room with the client, I often accept the myth. I rationalize that this is no time for me to muck about in my own problems; I've got enough to do trying to understand the client. And I believe it partly out of garden-variety defensiveness and narcissism.

Now the problem here, as you have no doubt already seen, is that my indignant hurt is not likely to go away if I just try to ignore it. It's eventually going to cause me trouble, which is to say it's going to cause my client trouble. Perhaps unconsciously I will wait for a chance to hurt my client back, however subtly. Or, more likely, I will twist myself out of shape trying to show what an empathic therapist I am. Of course, like most of my fellow therapists, I am too conscientious to do such things knowingly. But I would certainly be likely to do them, nonetheless.

Another client, one I saw some years ago, came to see me because of a recurrent need to sabotage himself whenever success seemed imminent. As I listened to his family history, I felt myself particularly moved and saddened by one part of his story. As far back as he could remember, he had been aware that there was something wrong with his younger brother. The boy had a very hard time in school, and it finally became clear to my client that his brother was retarded. It was also clear that his brother was the most loving person he knew and his best friend. My client went on to become a professional with graduate degrees, but in seeking to advance his career, he managed regularly to snatch defeat from the jaws of victory.

As he told me his story, I heard many elements that could have been, and later turned out to be, contributions to his rejection of success. But the one that stood out for me was the sad feeling of leaving his beloved brother farther and farther behind. It's not surprising that I focused on the brother; my younger sister was born severely brain-damaged and has been in an institution most of her life. Among my feelings concerning my sister are a great deal of sadness and also a considerable amount of survivor guilt.

As I look back on my work with that client, I am grateful that my own conflicts so quickly directed my attention to *his* survivor guilt, an area that turned out to be very fruitful.

It could have gone another way. I could easily have felt so much unconscious anxiety when an area of considerable personal pain was stirred up that, in the interests of self-protection, I blinded myself to the importance of my client's relationship with his brother.

Two Hidden Dramas

The depth psychologists have taught us that much of what goes on in the minds of our clients—and of everyone else—is hidden to them. Each person's history, each person's deepest wishes, impulses, and fears, lie out of sight. Nonetheless, they powerfully influence the person's behaviors and conscious attitudes. According to the depth psychologists, this influence works as strongly in the therapist as in the client. Thus, in addition to the visible, rational relationship unfolding in the consulting room, two hidden dramas are being played out in complex interaction: that of the client's psyche and that of the therapist's.

We have seen what a leading role the therapist plays in the client's drama and how the unconscious templates of the client's history shape the events of the relationship and the characteristics of the therapist into a never-ending kaleidoscope of feelings and thoughts about the therapy and the therapist.

A few years after Freud described the phenomenon of transference, he noted that something similar happens in the therapist with regard to the client. To this phenomenon Freud gave the name *countertransference,* and he saw it as an obstacle.[1] His ideal was the absolutely objective observer whose attention hovered evenly over the associations of the client, and who kept personal concerns and problems far from the consulting room. When this ideal was not achieved, the therapy suffered. Later some of Freud's followers began to question this view; certainly countertransference was often detrimental to the client and to the therapy, but it also seemed that sometimes the process taught therapists something about the client's problems they could have learned no other way.[2]

That insight led to a new interest in the study of countertransference. Gradually therapists came to recognize that no matter how much personal therapy they had had, no matter how "well analyzed" they might be, two complex dramas were inevitably played out in every consulting room, and one of them was going on in the unconscious of the therapist. It seemed clear that the more aware the therapist was of this fact, the safer the client would be, and the richer the therapist's sources of information.[3]

That understanding of countertransference was one of the conceptual roots of *intersubjective* theory. The image of two unconscious dramas being played out in the consulting room is essentially the same as the model of the therapy situation as a series of events organized by each of the two participants according to his or her unconscious templates and repetitions. Two of the great values of the intersubjective perspective are (1) its emphasis on the therapist's contribution to the therapy situation and (2) its demand for skepticism about the therapist's view of the situation. Both of these contributions come from the increasing sophistication with which therapists grasp the ubiquity and the power of countertransference.

Sources of Countertransference

The history of countertransference theory is filled with controversy about how that word should be defined.[4] *Countertransference* is now commonly considered to encompass *all* of the therapist's feelings and attitudes toward the client. Countertransference responses may take four forms:

1. *Realistic responses.* Some countertransference responses may be realistic. We should note here that an intersubjectivist never assumes he or she sees the world the way it is. With that caveat firmly in mind, however, we must recognize that some people tend to evoke similar responses from a wide variety of others. For example:

The client is a friendly and attractive person, and I feel positive toward her. Most therapists would be likely to feel this way, regardless of their personal history or conflicts.

The client is belligerent and somewhat threatening. I feel cautious and a bit frightened.

2. *Responses to transference.* Some countertransference feelings are responses to the client's transference; for example:

Acting out a transference, the client is seductive, and I feel excited—or perhaps frightened.

The client is flattering, and I feel inflated.

The client is critical, and I feel threatened.

3. *Responses to material troubling to the therapist.* Some countertransference feelings arise when a client

explores an area particularly troubling to the therapist; for example:

The client expresses anxiety about homosexuality. If I haven't come to terms with my own sex-identity issues, I may well share the client's anxiety.

I am going through a divorce. Hearing of the client's happy marriage, I feel envious.

4. *Characteristic responses of the therapist.* Some countertransference feelings are ones I take everywhere with me, so of course they accompany me into the consulting room, no matter what the client does:

Some men feel more or less competitive with every man they meet. Some of them are therapists.

Some people need to be liked or admired by everyone they meet. Some of those people are therapists, too.

Earlier I described a client's criticism of my lack of empathy. My hurt feelings were primarily an instance of the second type: a response to transference. They also had some elements of the fourth type: The therapist's characteristic response. I don't take well to criticism, wherever it comes from.

My identification with the client with the retarded brother is primarily an instance of the third type: he brought up an area that is conflictual for me. A sensitive therapist without my history could have picked up the brother's importance; then the countertransference would be considered to be of the first type: a realistic response.

My response to my client's criticism might well have hurt him. My response to the information about the damaged sibling was of value to the client. Here, then, are two good reasons for paying close attention to those feelings.

First, awareness of the countertransference will help us to protect our clients. Second, this awareness will enable us to profit from the insights these feelings can give us about the client.

Obstructive and Useful Countertransference

Heinrich Racker, in his influential book *Transference and Countertransference*, classifies countertransference phenomena as either obstructive or useful.*

An *obstructive* countertransference phenomenon is one that interferes with the therapist's clarity and empathy. Had my own intolerable guilt and anxiety about my sister caused me to turn the exploration away from the retarded brother, my countertransference feelings would have been obstructive.

Useful countertransference feelings and attitudes are those that an alert therapist succeeds in employing to the client's advantage by continuing to observe and ponder them until they become empathic insights. An example is the sadness stirred in me by the story of my client's retarded brother. My hurt feelings about being criticized by the client I particularly liked could have been useful countertransference had I accepted them and recognized that they indicated how much he needed to hurt me just then.

An important point to note here is that at every moment our deep characterological, habitual responses lie in wait for us, looking for an opportunity to express themselves as countertransference. This is our old friend

---

*Actually Racker calls useful and obstructive countertransference *concordant* and *complimentary*, respectively. These terms are confusing if the reader doesn't have a command of object relations vocabulary, so I'm using *useful* and *obstructive*.

the repetition compulsion: just like our clients, each of us has a history that is always eager to make itself known. We have seen that this compulsion in our clients provides a powerful therapeutic opportunity; in therapists it is a trap to be looked for vigilantly. What kept me from coolly using my hurt feelings as a useful countertransference was the pressure of my lifelong fear of criticism. I was able to use my feelings about the retarded brother because my sadness and guilt were not strong enough to swamp my empathy and take me off the job.

Obstructive countertransference

Obstructive countertransference phenomena expose us to several dangers:

1. Countertransference can blind us to an important area of exploration. Conversely, it can cause us to focus on an area that is more our issue than the client's.

From time to time the client hints at an emerging sexual fantasy. The therapist has his own anxieties about that aspect of sexuality and successfully keeps himself from seeing its importance to the client.

The therapist has serious unresolved conflicts about her relationship with her mother. She significantly overemphasizes this aspect of the client's dynamics and so influences the client to overemphasize it.

2. Countertransference can cause us to use our clients for vicarious gratification.

A therapist with conflicts about his own dependency feelings may subtly urge the client toward (superficial) independent actions as a vicarious way of trying to overcome his own dependence. As a result, the client's conflicts become more hidden instead of more available. This sort of development can occur in any area that personally troubles the therapist.

The therapist may be tempted to urge the client toward more sexual freedom. Increased sexual freedom may well be a good thing for many clients. And surely many therapists have less sexual freedom than they would like. Those therapists can easily be tempted to deal with that lack vicariously. There are many reasons why a therapist should be very cautious about imposing opinions and advice on clients; this is a major one.

3. Countertransference can lead us to emit subtle cues that greatly influence the client. We sometimes forget how important we are to our clients. Consciously and unconsciously our clients tune their receivers to us. They miss precious little, neither changes in facial expression, shifts in posture, tone of voice, nor muscle tension. There is no way the therapist can (or should!) control all these cues. The cues will be transmitted, and many of them will be received and interpreted.

If unconsciously I need a certain client (or all my clients!) to like and admire me, however earnestly I claim to welcome the expression of negative feelings toward me, the client is likely to perceive unconsciously the thousand tiny cues that reveal how I really respond to anger or criticism. Psychologists who study learning phenomena have established that the unconscious reception of such subtle cues can quickly shape a subject's behavior. If I do not find some way to reduce the intensity of that neurotic need, I am in danger of teaching my clients to emphasize their friendly feelings toward me and suppress the not-so-friendly ones.

If I am erotically attracted to a client, I may transmit a host of seductive messages that could, to say the least, leave the client considerably confused about our relationship.

Every client (except ones the therapist really doesn't like) probably stirs two competing sets of feelings in the therapist: therapists want to liberate their clients and send them on their way, and they want to keep them dependent. (This ambivalence appears in practically all parents as well.) If they're not vigilant, therapists will find ways to send conflicting cues to their clients.

4. Countertransference can lead us to make interventions that are not in the client's interest.

If I feel wounded by a client, I may, as we have seen, find a way to hurt the client, all the while sincerely believing I am making the best therapeutic move.

If the client's history with his father stirs my own unresolved anger at *my* father, I am in danger of saying critical and angry things about the client's father. Even with the purest of intentions, hostile criticism of the client's family is probably not good practice; motivated by countertransference, it can be destructive.

The client speaks mostly trivia. Kohut has taught us how important it is to look past the defensive trivia to the client's fear. The therapist is then in a position to empathize with the client. But if the client's chatter has stirred countertransference feelings of irritation and impatience, the therapist will be tempted to focus on the trivia and miss the underlying fear. Then the therapist's intervention ("It seems you're avoiding the things that really concern you") will be heard as criticism, and the client's underlying fear will be strengthened rather than reduced.

5. Countertransference can lead us to adopt the roles into which the client's transference casts us.

If a client persistently accuses a therapist of being nonempathic and hostile, pressures will eventually mount in the therapist to treat the client just that way. The very intensity of those pressures can teach a great deal about the client if the therapist manages to resist them. The danger, of course, is that they will be too difficult to resist; and if, in addition, the therapist has buried hostility looking for expression, he is likely to give the client a hard time indeed until he frees himself from the hypnotic pressures.

Educated and intelligent and proud of the fact, the client subtly establishes the implication that we are two wise and special people talking it all over. This client provides the therapist with a variety of unconscious temptations: playing such a role is easier than doing therapy, and besides, the role is flattering. If the therapist accepts the bait, the client has executed an effective defensive maneuver.

The client treats the therapist like a wise elder who understands the world better than the client and whose advice and opinion are very valuable. I hardly need say how tempting it can be to accept this role.

When a client sees the therapist as absolutely wonderful—that is, when the client is in the throes of an idealizing transference—the therapist's equanimity is sorely tested. Either or both of two temptations are likely to appear: the therapist may start to make self-deprecating remarks out of embarrassment, or, secretly preening, may start to act out the role of supertherapist.

A female client has a strong positive transference, to which her male therapist responds with pleasure and gratification. At a certain point in the therapy, the client's sexual interest in her husband reawakens. The therapist consciously sees this development as progress. But unconsciously he feels loss, as well as jealousy of the husband. He is likely then to transmit cues of irritation and sulkiness. If she then redirects her energy toward the therapist (perhaps because she has picked up the cues), the therapist is likely to feel guilty toward the husband.*

Projective Identification

If the client's attempt to influence the therapist to accept these roles is sufficiently powerful, the pressures on the therapist to comply may become overwhelming. For historical reasons that need not concern us here, the client is then said to be transmitting a *projective identification.*[5] (Since clients are almost always trying to influence the therapist to some degree, it is useful to reserve the term for instances the therapist experiences as intense and compelling.) When the attempt to influence the therapist in this way is successful, the therapist is said to experience an *introjective identification* or *projective counteridentification.* The pressure can be as intense as hypnotic induction, and after succumbing to it and acting out the role, therapists can find themselves as bewildered as if they had just carried out a posthypnotic suggestion.[6]

Projective identification takes two main forms.

1. The client may want to project onto the therapist feelings too difficult for the client to own. The client will then attempt to induce the therapist to experience

---

*This example and several others in this chapter have been taken from or inspired by Racker's *Transference and Countertransference* (n. 3) and Tansey and Burke's *Understanding Countertransference* (n. 4).

these feelings. If the projective identification is successful, the therapist then feels the way he imagines the client feels; that is, he *identifies with* that aspect of the client.

A client of mine found himself in a severe conflict between his desire for his wife and his attraction to a woman he had just met. As we worked together, I became more and more convinced that he really loved his wife and would end by staying with her. Suddenly, without warning, he told his wife he wanted a divorce, left her, and went to the other woman. My first reactions were shock and some dismay. Then over the next few weeks I began to feel terribly guilty. I thought he had made a serious mistake and that it was my fault. If I had done better work with him, he would have untangled the unconscious pressures and made a better choice. I talked the situation over with a wise colleague, who asked me if the client were in touch with any guilt about walking out on his wife. I said apparently not, and then suddenly the lights went on. Somehow my client had induced me to take on his guilt, and I had done so with a vengeance. As gently and gradually as I could manage, I suggested he might consider that perhaps he had some guilt feelings. Processing his projective identification (that is, my *introjective identification*) enabled me to pick up a major theme that I had missed.

2. A client wants to cast the therapist in the role of a significant other person and uncover an internal relationship too difficult to access in any other way. The client attempts to induce in the therapist the feelings of the significant other.

A woman client who had been sexually abused by her father from the age of 8 to 18 was working with a male therapist. She felt rage and guilt toward her father, but only numbness toward her mother. After a long period of therapy in which she never expressed negative feelings toward the therapist, she suddenly vented a wild outburst of negativity.

"I come in here week after week begging for help. You have no idea at all how hard it is for me. Everywhere I turn, people are fucking me over—my husband, my boss, the other workers. You never say anything to guide me. All you do is sit there, calm and cool. You have to do something."

The therapist panicked and froze. He found himself feeling helpless and afraid she would commit suicide. He sought consultation.

His consultant helped him see that his client had cast him in the role of her mother, who had just sat there while her father literally fucked her over. Her repressed rage at her mother had been a serious obstacle to her progress. Now the door was open and her rage was available for exploration.

Thomas Ogden, one of the most lucid writers on projective identification, describes the phenomenon this way:

If we imagine for a moment that the patient is both the director and one of the principal actors in the interpersonal enactment of an internal object relationship, and that the therapist is an unwitting actor in the same drama, then projective identification is the process whereby the therapist is given stage directions for a particular role. In this analogy it must be borne in mind that the therapist has not volunteered to play a part and only retrospectively comes to understand that he has been playing a role in the patient's enactment of an aspect of his inner world.[7]

Useful countertransference

Having examined the dangers of countertransference, let's now brighten the picture by seeing how countertransference can be beneficial. Countertransference is closely related to empathy. You will recall that we have defined countertransference as *all* of the therapist's responses to the client; thus it follows that all empathy begins with a countertransference response. Let's consider the necessary conditions for the production of empathy.

First, it seems clear that the only countertransference that is a potential generator of empathy is the countertransference stimulated by the client, not one that the therapist takes everywhere. Second, once the countertransference feeling or attitude has arisen, it becomes therapeutic empathy when the therapist can maintain or achieve an *optimal distance* from the feeling. So it must not be repressed, but neither must it be permitted to swamp the therapist, either with obstructive impulses (to fight back, say) or with burdensome identification (such as feeling too sad to be effective). It needs to be held at a distance that permits a *felt* understanding of the client but does not overwhelm the therapist. Let's look at some examples.

A male client says, "I understand that [the name of another therapist] left her husband and is with a new man." The (female) therapist feels a surge of excitement. As she examines it, she realizes it comes from the very warm feeling she has for this client. But why would his remark excite her? The thought occurs to her that he might have fantasies about *her* going to a new man. She waits a moment and then asks him if he has any thoughts about the other therapist's new man.

Laughing, the client responds, "I wondered if he had been a client of hers." The therapist is now in a position to explore the transference implications of his remark.

A male client speaks of women in ways that the female therapist hears as degrading. After several such remarks, her objectivity erodes, and she finds herself increasingly angry. It occurs to her that the client could not be unaware of the effect such remarks were likely to have on a female therapist—or, for that matter, on any other woman. Her anger subsides as she becomes interested in the question why he would want to offend her and push her away. She now has the information to explore an aspect of the relationship previously hidden from her.

As the client eloquently and dramatically spins out his story, the therapist becomes aware that he is beginning to feel like the audience at a tragic romantic drama. It isn't just the drama that makes him feel that way. It's also his distinct impression that the client wants nothing from him but his presence as a rapt audience. At first he finds himself enjoying the role. It's easy work, and the client is indeed entertaining. Then slowly he realizes he is feeling lonely and useless. When the therapist questions him, the client says he is quite satisfied; he really needs to have his story heard, and he greatly appreciates the attentive listening he is receiving. The therapist's feeling of loneliness deepens and becomes somewhat distressing. And then one day he is struck by a strong hunch. Is it possible, he wonders, that the client is showing him what it was like for him as a child, that one or both of his parents were so addicted to narcissistic display that the only available role for a child was that of a rapt (and terribly lonely) audience? A new way of understanding and exploring the client's pain is opened to him.

For the past few months the therapy has bogged down in the client's resistance. The client reports feelings of anger and mistrust toward the therapist. The impasse seems impenetrable. One day the therapist realizes that her feelings at the very beginning and very end of the hour are different from the discouragement she feels during most of the session. When the client greets her and when he says good-bye, she feels warm and connected to him. This response appears to be in marked contrast to his reported anger and mistrust. It begins to seem to her that at the beginning and end of the session she is receiving subtle messages of affection, perhaps of love.

Therapist:	I've been feeling a warm connection with you at the beginning and end of our sessions. I wonder if you've noticed anything like that.
Client:	Well, sometimes it seems I don't feel mistrustful till we get settled down.
Therapist:	Well, how do you feel toward me when you first come in and we say hello?
Client:	(*pondering*) I feel good. I feel like I like you. The mistrust seems to start a bit later.
Therapist:	It feels to me at those times that you like me a lot.
Client:	(*uncomfortably*) That might be right.

Therapist:	We've been stuck at a roadblock for some time.
Client:	We certainly have.
Therapist:	Do you think maybe that's because liking me so much seems dangerous to you?
	(*The client is silent, eyes downcast. When he looks up, his eyes are filled with tears.*)
Therapist:	I can certainly understand how scary that is. (*And the impasse is broken.*)

The Therapist's Difficulties

For the therapist, remaining aware of the countertransference is often the most difficult task of all. We want to be objective and neutral. We want our feelings for the client to be our servants, not our masters. We more than *want* control over our feelings; we demand it of ourselves. We think of ourselves as professionals who keep our desires and anxieties out of our work.

It does not fit my self-image to allow my feelings to be hurt by a client.

It fits it even less to know I want to punish or make love to a client.

I do not like to think of myself as one who finds some clients particularly appealing and some particularly distasteful.

Nor do I like to think of myself as one who can be charmed, repelled, or intimidated out of continuing to steer a steady course.

No matter how much admiration my ego craves in the rest of my life, I expect that where my clients are concerned, I can say with the Buddhists, "Praise and blame are all the same."

But the truth is that I am probably never for a moment free of one or more of those pressures. Much of the time they are mild enough so that even though I am unaware of them, they do no harm. Sometimes I manage to pay attention to them, and then I learn a great deal about my client and our relationship. Sometimes I go to a colleague for help and discover that I am caught by a destructive set of feelings toward the client, and I have to extricate myself, sometimes with great pain and difficulty. And I have to remind myself continually that it simply is not true that there is one person in this room doing transference and one maintaining a firm grip on objective reality.

The Need for Vigilance

Of all the reasons for paying attention to the forces of countertransference, probably none is more important than the need to avoid treating the client in the way that caused the original wounds. We have seen the power of the forces that propel the client toward recreating in the therapy all significant childhood relationships, including those that caused the trouble in the first place. That phenomenon, transference, is one of the most powerful tools the therapist–client team has at its disposal. And we have seen that in order to use that tool for the client's growth and liberation, the therapist has to respond to the transference in ways that differ from the original responses the client received. When my client sees me as a punishing father and resents me accordingly, it is crucial that I don't respond the way the client's father responded long ago. That is a sure way to reopen the wound. And the laws of countertransference dictate that I will sometimes feel strong pressure to respond in just that way. It will greatly profit my clients if I remind myself at frequent intervals to keep a vigilant countertransference watch posted.

The purpose of increasing one's awareness of countertransference forces is not to eliminate countertransference. Any effort to do so would be like trying to eliminate the unconscious. It can't be done, nor should it be, since countertransference is the source of empathy. The goal is merely to shorten the time it takes to recognize and resolve a countertransference attitude or impulse. Inevitably, a vast array of feelings, wishes, and fears are going to cascade through us in the presence of each client. Inevitably, we will not always be able to identify them at once and use them to increase our understanding of the relationship. And it is probably equally inevitable that from time to time we will get caught in a countertransference that will burden the therapy and set it back. That is all part of the process.

What we can work to do is to shorten the time required to see what we're up to. The more vigilant we become (I would like to say the more *gently* vigilant we become) about our own attitudes, our own feelings and impulses, our own wishes and fears, the more quickly we will be able to turn the countertransference to the therapy's advantage.

(7)

The Therapist's
Dilemmas

〜

One question arises again and again for every therapist: What should I *give* this client at this moment? As we will see, this question leads to some dilemmas. Nonetheless, some answers seem clear. Though we cannot always do all that we expect of ourselves, we have a pretty good idea of some of the things that we *should* give:

We should always give our clients our full attention and energy.

We should make our best effort to *understand* them—to understand what they are experiencing at the present moment and to understand the themes of their lives, both apparent and subtle, as they unfold before us.

We should let them *know* that they are indeed with someone who is trying hard to understand them.

We should give them the safety and freedom to reveal anything they wish, without fear of being judged.

And we should give them the certainty that they are with an ethical professional who knows the boundaries and will not cross them.

Having said that, each of us is left with an extremely difficult question: How much of myself should I reveal to the client?

How much of my personal life do I talk about?

How free am I to tell clients my feelings about them? That is, when I am aware of a countertransference feeling or attitude, do I discuss it?

How am I to communicate warmth and caring?

What do I do when I find myself guilty of a failure of empathy? Do I acknowledge it? Do I say how I feel about it?

These are among the most complex and interesting questions for the next generation of clinicians to explore and expand upon. I dare say no one really knows the best answers to them. We have seen how puzzled Rogers became when he tried to figure out just how far genuineness should extend. It is likely that we will never find firm answers that work for every client and every situation. What seems important is that we think through the implications of each strategy we explore, that we pay attention to the effects on the client, and above all, that we scrupulously consider whether what we do is for the client or for ourselves.

The Conservative-to-Radical Continuum

We can begin to explore these questions by thinking of the possible answers as falling along a continuum from conservative to radical.

At the right end is the classic psychoanalytic position: therapy is a one-way encounter. The therapist is to lie as low as possible and give nothing but interpretations.[1] We have looked at the excesses of this position and found it one that few modern therapists outside the most conservative psychoanalytic institutes care to adopt. But it has unmistakable advantages. Foremost among them is the protection it affords against the therapist's acting out the countertransference. One of the slogans heard around the Boston Psychoanalytic Institute some years ago was "The analyst's orthodoxy is the patient's protection." There was something to that. Another bit of wisdom passed around that same institute, one I have held dear for years, was "There are only two ways to do real damage to patients: *seducing them* and *punishing them*. If you do neither of those things, you can't get into serious trouble." (*Seducing* meant much more than literally seducing them; it meant working to arouse their desire for you, their admiration for you, or their dependence on you. *Punishing* meant anything, however subtle, calculated to hurt them.) We are less likely to let ourselves slip into acting seductively or punitively if we are restrained by stringent guidelines.

This position has the additional advantage of giving the therapist a clear, consistent guideline. You never have to wonder: Should I answer that question? Should I share this feeling? The answer is comfortably and forever no.

At the left, or radical, end of the continuum we'll put the encounter therapists.[2] Encounter therapy flourished in certain American subcultures during the 1960s and '70s. It is much less common now, but it has left its mark. The encounter therapists operate on the principle that the client's problem is inauthenticity and that a completely open relationship will be therapeutic. The encounter is entirely two-way. Encounter therapists reveal every feeling they have about their clients and disclose themselves as fully as they expect the clients to do. The only limits to the depth, breadth, and form of intimacy are those of the therapist's sense of ethics.

Whatever the excesses of this form of therapy, it too has its advantages. Like classical psychoanalysis, it has the virtue of consistency. The encounter therapist never has to wonder: Should I? The answer is always yes. It has another virtue as well: it attempts to be as egalitarian as possible, thus reducing the power imbalance between therapist and client.

Where do the therapists we have considered fall on this self-disclosure continuum? It seems clear that they all moved to the left as their careers progressed, coming more and more to trust their spontaneity and to express their human warmth. Neither Rogers nor Kohut was certain where to locate the optimal point on the continuum. Gill's final position was somewhat farther to the right than Rogers' and Kohut's, although his recommendation that therapists permit themselves warmth and spontaneity shows him to be much more liberal than his analytic forebears.

Any therapist who does not have the comfort and security of being ensconced at either end of the continuum has to face the fact that the questions of self-disclosure present real dilemmas.

Self-Disclosure: Too Little or Too Much?

Rogers, Gill, and Kohut take a moderately conservative position on how much the therapist should disclose. All stress that it is most helpful if the therapy is about the client, not the therapist. Gill and Kohut strongly imply that the therapist who answers personal questions robs the client of an opportunity to explore the feelings and fantasies that gave rise to the question.

A client of mine once became occupied with the question of my sexual orientation, and in session after session asked me to tell him if I was straight or gay. It is a question I sometimes answer, particularly at the beginning of therapy, when the client is trying to decide whether I'm the right therapist. But in this case I decided not to answer the question and told him in as open and friendly a manner as I could muster that I thought it would be better for his therapy if I were not to answer it. He returned to it repeatedly. When the therapy ended he made a special point of telling me that, although my refusal to answer his question had been frustrating for him, in the end he was glad I had made that choice. It had given him a chance to go progressively deeper into his fantasies about me, into his hopes and fears about me, and into his complex feelings about his own sexual orientation. He thought that if I had answered the question, he would have felt satisfied and dropped the subject with relief, having managed to avoid what turned out to be an important area of exploration.

The opposite view, of course, is that an easy "no big deal" policy of modest amounts of self-revelation tends to demystify the therapist and the therapeutic process and therefore has advantages. It makes the therapist seem more human, and it reduces a bit the painful imbalance of self-disclosure that is entirely one-way. Also, Kohut reminds us, it is always costly to deal the client an unnecessary rejection. That is a persuasive argument. Nonetheless, I continue to hold the conservative position. It is important to consider carefully the possible cost of much self-disclosure; that is, it can reduce the opportunity for the client's valuable exploration of fantasy. Probably no one position on this continuum fits all clients and all situations. Each situation is unique, and each client probably profits from an individual approach to this question.

I have found these guidelines helpful:

1. I try not to make a fetish out of not talking about myself. If a client, on the way out the door, asks in a friendly and casual way, "Where are you going on your vacation?" I tell where I'm going. If the client were then to probe, however ("Who are you going with? Are you married?"), I would be likely to respond, "Ah . . . maybe we'd better talk about that next time."

2. When I refuse to answer a question, I try hard not to look as though I were playing "I've got a secret, so I'm one up on you." I explain as fully as I can why I am taking this stand. If I think my response frustrates or angers by client, I say I can understand that reaction very well. Analysands of my generation were driven wild by the psychoanalyst's silence in the face of any question at all. None of our authors is recommending that we put our clients through that ordeal.

Disclosing Feelings

As a therapist, I must decide if it's ever helpful to disclose my feelings about the client, and if so, under what conditions.

Positive regard

To Rogers, it was essential that the therapist not only feel positive regard but communicate it to the client as well. There is more than one way of communicating it.

1. I can explicitly state my positive regard. Therapists do indeed say to clients, "I like you," "I love you," "I find you interesting," "I think you're very attractive," "I think you'd be very good at that job," and so on.

2. I can *imply* positive regard by the way I act with the client. The way the therapist listens can demonstrate a sincere effort to understand. By the quality of my posture, facial expression, and tone of voice, I can communicate a basic regard for the client that is constant through the vagaries of superficial human changeability.

In trying to decide whether it's best to communicate positive regard by what you say or by what you do, it is worth pondering why it's important to communicate it at all. One reason is that it's probably not possible to form a therapeutic alliance without communicating positive regard. Another reason is that with most clients a major therapeutic goal is an increase in secure self-esteem. Everything the therapist does is ultimately meant to contribute to this goal, and the communication of positive regard is an important means of doing so.

How is positive regard best communicated? Let's look at the problems that can arise when we voice it explicitly.

There is, first of all, the question of sincerity. A client could be forgiven for wondering if statements of affection and esteem are little more than what therapists say to all their clients. That problem seems to recede when therapists communicate positive regard by what they do and the way they do it, rather than by what they say. I confess to a personal prejudice here; it seems to me that sometimes words are cheap, and that real regard is communicated by subtle cues and by actual behaviors.

It's a safe bet that when clients ask, directly or indirectly, if their therapists like them, they are doing a good deal more than asking that question. They are telling their therapists something important about a lack of secure self-esteem. The requested reassurance may provide temporary relief, but it does not address the underlying issue. And the most serious danger of providing that temporary relief is that it momentarily takes the energy out of the client's concern, and a valuable opportunity may be lost: the opportunity for the client to get in touch with the emotions and the memories that surround this issue.

So if, directly or indirectly, clients raise the question of my feelings about them, I *don't* tell them I like them, love them, or find them interesting. I let them know how thoroughly I understand the importance this topic holds for them. I do my best to give them every chance to explore the hopes, fears, and fantasies that generate such a question, and the feelings evoked by my evasion of a direct answer. I explain that I believe this exploration can be of great value to them, since it can give them access to the experiences and resulting attitudes that interfere with their self-esteem, and that it can ultimately enhance that self-esteem more strongly and more lastingly than could any momentary reassurance from me.

Sometimes I need to decline to answer a question about my feelings toward the client. At such times I console myself with the knowledge that my clients probably know more about my attitudes toward them than I do, anyway. For months or years they have been watching me, listening to me, gauging my tone of voice, following the changes in my eyes, noticing when I look sad and concerned, and when and how I smile or laugh. I know only my conscious feelings and attitudes; they, I suspect, know much more.

The therapeutic relationship is effective to the extent that clients are relatively free to explore and express their feelings, free of the inevitable concerns that characterize normal social intercourse. When I am trying to tell a friend my feelings, it's hard enough to stay in touch with those feelings and their changes. That task is made considerably harder by the fact that I have to concern myself with my friend's feelings, too. Everything I say is going to affect my friend, and each of those changes will in turn cause new changes in me. Furthermore, I am likely to censor those feelings that I anticipate will stir something in my friend that I am not willing to deal with. Thus, most nontherapy situations are not calculated to maximize one's abilities to learn about one's feelings and to risk sharing them. The therapeutic situation can be different. Presented not with an array of changeable feelings but rather with the constancy of the therapist's presence, clients can deal more easily with their own changing feelings.

Further, the therapeutic relationship is unique in that clients are encouraged to explore the far reaches of their wishes, impulses, fears, and fantasies—to go beyond what is "realistic" or what is acceptable in a normal relationship. I think therapists help that exploration by maintaining a relatively constant posture of accepting, empathic interest and not adding the confusion of their own inevitably fluctuating feelings. Here is an illustration:

Client: I really like you. (*expectant pause*)

Therapist: (*nodding warmly*) I do hear that. (*pause*) Can you tell me how you're feeling now?

Client: (*uncomfortably*) It feels bad in a way to say something like that to you and not have you really respond to it.

Therapist: (*nodding*) Can you tell me more about that?

Client: Well, it's not just that I like you. (*pause*) You're very important to me, and I have no idea how you feel about me. It's weird that you're so important to me and for all I know I'm just one more client to you.

Therapist: I can really understand that. It certainly must seem weird, and very frustrating, too. (*pause*) Could you tell me if you have some ideas about how I might feel about you?

Client: You seem very friendly and I guess you like me OK.

Therapist: Sounds like that really isn't enough.

Client: I guess in some ways it really isn't.

Therapist: Could you tell me what *would* be enough?

Client: Oh, I don't know. Maybe nothing would really be enough. I think what I really want is to be the most important person in your whole world. I'd like it if you thought about me when I wasn't here, and if you missed me. I know that's silly, isn't it?

Therapist: It most certainly is not silly. It's very understandable. I can see how important it is to you.

And the way is open for the therapist to empathize and, if the therapy has reached that stage, to help the client see the connection between this need and early deprivations.

Had the therapist responded to the first "I really like you" with "I like you, too," I think it would have been more difficult for this client to become aware of the extremity of his need. It would have seemed to him like a familiar relationship in which two people exchange protestations of affection. And it would have seemed inappropriate to explore just how strong the need was.

The existential psychotherapists discuss the pros and cons of explicit statements of positive regard. To them the goal is to enable clients to accept responsibility for their lives, which includes control over their self-image. Therapists don't achieve this goal by expressing acceptance, love, or admiration for their clients. Indeed, the existential psychotherapists say, such professions could lead to passivity and dependency in clients, reinforcing the belief that their self-image is dependent on other people's admiration and acceptance. Existentialist psychologists do believe, however, that under certain circumstances a therapist's compassionate acceptance can be the *precondition* for the client's coming to self-acceptance.[3]

This position seems to accord with Kohut's stance of empathizing with the client who has a need for mirroring, rather than being the mirror and saying the client is indeed the fairest one of all. In fact, Kohut may have provided the means for therapists to help clients toward this goal of the existentialists. If I am courageously to assume responsibility for and control over my self-image (and my destiny as well), perhaps I need to know that someone has really understood the depth of my dependency and has grasped the pain of the early deprivations that generated it.

Let me quickly acknowledge that my position here is controversial. Many wise therapists, among them many of Kohut's students, think there are times when it is important to tell clients how much you care for them. These therapists pick such times carefully and speak out only when they think an avowal of affection will evoke a valuable response. Theirs is an entirely defensible position; few rules work every time.

Negative feelings

What do you do about your anger or boredom or feelings of distance? Do you share those feelings? Rogers and his followers have a clear and convincing position on this question:

1. Do *not* share each passing irritation.

2. Consider sharing a negative feeling only if it is striking or persistent or is interfering with your capacity to be fully present with the client.

3. Before expressing a negative feeling, ask yourself this question: For whom am I doing this? Do I want to unburden myself, to get revenge, to hurt the client? Do I want to demonstrate how authentic I am? If the answer to any of those questions is yes, keep the feeling to yourself or save it for your supervisor.

4. If it seems to you that your speaking out is indeed meant for the benefit of the client and the movement of the therapy, say what you have to say in a manner that shows your basic regard. And say it in a way that minimizes the chance that the client will hear it as criticism. Place responsibility for your negative feeling on yourself, not on the client. Rogers would never have said, "I find you boring today." He might have said, "I'm distressed to find that I'm not very interested in our session today, and it makes me very uncomfortable to tell

you this. I think the boredom comes from my not feeling really connected with you. Do you have any idea
what's happening between us today that's making me
feel this way?"[4]

Failures of Empathy

What should therapists do when they find themselves
guilty of a failure of empathy? Should they acknowledge
it? Should they say how they feel about it?

Kohut taught that such failures are of great value to the
client; they are what make transmuting internalization
possible. So to begin with, we are certainly to empathize
with the client's *experience* of having been mistreated or
misunderstood by us, whether or not we think we are
guilty. And it seems equally noncontroversial to follow
Gill's advice to validate the perception and affirm the plausibility of the client's interpretation. "I think you're quite
right—I wasn't as warm as usual when you arrived today.
. . . And it seems quite plausible to me that you'd interpret
that as indicating I don't like you as much today. I can
really see how you'd read it that way." Now we enter a
controversial area: Does one go on to explore whether or
not one *is* feeling less friendly toward the client today?
Gill's position is clear: the therapist *never* denies a feeling.
Knowing that everyone has an unconscious, the therapist
at most admits no *awareness* of such a feeling (if, indeed,
the therapist has no awareness of it).

But what if in fact the therapist is liking the client less
today? Gill's (somewhat tentative) position is that sharing
such a feeling is not useful, for reasons examined in Chapter 4. But what is the therapist to do? If, indeed, I am not
feeling good about the client, and if that client detects my
attitude long before I have decided it's a feeling worth

sharing, is there any honorable, authentic way to avoid dealing with my antipathy? I think not. At this point it must be shared, with all the caution and gentleness that Rogers teaches us.

Now what if I come to think I have made an *error* that has resulted in a failure of empathy, such as interrupting or criticizing the client or failing to follow the client's lead? Do I confess the error? Kohut is our most valuable guide here. Though he doesn't deal with this question explicitly, his implication is clear: we do whatever maximizes the client's capacity to make use of our failure, whatever will best enable the transmuting internalization to take place. There isn't much doubt that acknowledging the error (without breast-beating) is helpful. Of all the types of self-disclosure we are considering, this seems the one that offers the least costly means to demystify ourselves, thus helping clients develop trust in us. If nondefensiveness is one of the main goals we strive for as therapists, this seems like a good way to practice it.

Intersubjectivity

Robert Stolorow, Bernard Brandchaft, and George Atwood, innovative students of both Gill and Kohut, introduce a valuable caution into considerations of these questions. They remind us that clients' original wounds came from their caretakers' repeated failures to validate and empathize with their reality. Thus they warn us, whatever choices we make, we must be wary of adopting a stance that seems to bestow on the therapist the prerogative to decide whether the client's psychic reality is indeed the reality:

> It is assumed that the patient's experience of the therapeutic relationship is always shaped both by inputs from the analyst

and by the structures of meaning into which these are assimi-
lated by the patient. . . . From this vantage point, the reality
of the patient's perception of the analyst is neither debated
nor confirmed. Instead, these perceptions serve as points of
departure for an exploration of the meanings and organizing
principles that structure the patient's psychic reality.[5]

Stolorow and his colleagues are major contributors to
the exploration of *intersubjectivity,* a perspective that has
important implications for the issues we are considering
here.[6] Our intellectual ancestors understandably began by
seeing the therapist as the detached, objective physician
who maintained a view of reality, while patients, under the
sway of transference, distorted their view of the therapist.
That understanding of the therapeutic relationship has
gradually evolved, and intersubjectivity is its most recent
form: both therapist and client view the ambiguous data of
the relationship through the lenses of their templates and
repetitions and thus choose their interpretations of those
data under the influence of unconscious forces. Stolorow
and his associates put it this way: As children, we must find
a way to organize the profusion of stimuli with which we
are confronted. Strongly influenced by our parents and
teachers and by earlier events in our lives, we form unconscious principles to organize current stimuli. Since these
principles operate outside of awareness, it seems to us we
are merely responding to the reality of any given situation.
When those principles don't serve us well in later years, we
go into therapy to bring them into consciousness, weaken
their hold on us, and give us new choices.

In Chapter 4 we met a man who could not feel both
tenderness and passion for the same woman. Stolorow
would say that his organizing principles were: (1) It is
forbidden to have sexual feelings for a nice woman. (2)
It is unworthy to have tender feelings for a sexy woman.
Since these principles are unconscious, his conscious

experience is that it is just this particular woman who does not excite him and that particular woman for whom he feels no tenderness.

Clients look at the therapist through the lenses of their principles, thus providing the therapist an opportunity to help them reflect on those principles. Therapists look at clients through the lenses of *their* principles. Though it seems unlikely that the therapist's principles will ever become conscious in their entirety, it is important for the therapist continually to strive to become more and more aware of them. One implication of the intersubjective view is that a premium is placed on the therapist's nondefensiveness.

Thus it is not meaningful to assert that some of a client's responses to the therapist are reality based and some reflect transference. They are all reality based, inasmuch as they begin with the actual stimulus complex that is the therapist. They all reflect transference, too, inasmuch as all perceptions are filtered through the organizing principles. Once that is understood, the client's responses to the therapist provide a rich opportunity to help the client examine and reflect upon his or her organizing principles.

As the intersubjective view gains influence, it is creating ferment in the development of our craft, and much of that ferment bears on these dilemmas. Many writers are suggesting that the intersubjective position implies that the therapist should be more spontaneous and expressive, which in turn implies more countertransference disclosure.[7] The rationale of these writers is that the classical therapist was thought to be (or at least hoped to be) in a position of detached objectivity. It seemed important for the classical therapist to give off that message: "Go ahead and let your fantasies roam. I'm watching the store." The reticent "neutrality" of the therapist was an intentional way of communicating that detached objectivity to the client. Now, say the intersubjectivists, we recognize that the therapist is neither detached nor entirely objective, and in the interest of honesty we might communicate that awareness by allowing ourselves greater freedom and spontaneity. Such freedom offers the client a more egalitarian relationship and conveys the intersubjective message that the therapist doesn't confidently *know* what's going on, but rather is there to collaborate with the client in *learning* what's going on. Thus, for instance, the intersubjectivists tend to share with their clients their own conflicts about how much of their feelings to reveal.

It is not just the intersubjectivists who are exploring the potential benefits of revealing countertransference feelings. Some writers in the classical psychoanalytic tradition are now teaching that countertransference disclosure may be the only way to break some impasses.[8] Recently, for example, a client I had worked with for many years and who had made remarkable life changes suddenly developed a powerful and intractable negative transference. I thought I understood it as an outgrowth of his current life situation and I certainly understood it as a result of his troubled relationship with his father. I explored these variables with him and searched for whatever changes he had perceived in me that had brought on this sudden anger and distrust. Nothing helped; he remained angry and distrustful and apparently now discounted our long-standing therapeutic alliance. Consonant with my conservative position on the disclosure continuum, I empathized with his feelings and said nothing about mine, which eventually became very strong indeed: I was badly hurt. Finally he ended the therapy and left. Later, reading Karen Maroda's "Power of Countertransference," I realized for the first time that had I told him how hurt and bewildered I was, I might have broken the impasse.

Thus it seems to me that the field of psychodynamic therapy is moving in the direction of greater spontaneity and greater countertransference disclosure. As it does so, I think it becomes ever more important to recognize that these new freedoms carry increased responsibility, that powerful instruments can also be dangerous weapons. Most of the proponents of the intersubjective view emphasize the need for considerable restraint in disclosing countertransference feelings. They recognize the possibility that the countertransference will be acted out in ways that could unwittingly wound the client again by playing into the client's familiar and destructive interpersonal scenarios. Though the relationship may be seen as an intersubjective one, it is important to remember that it is not symmetrical.

The new freedom of the intersubjective perspective does not relieve us of the necessity for discipline. Rather, it makes the therapist's discipline all the more important. The therapy is, after all, for the client's benefit, not the therapist's. The basic freedoms are the client's and the basic responsibilities are the therapist's. The therapist, then, must never lose sight of the questions: Am I making this choice for the client or to satisfy some need of mine? Am I co-creating a new and healing relationship, or am I being drawn into an old destructive one?

In my opinion, this new freedom is not for beginners. As one begins to practice this craft, it seems essential to learn to be very disciplined indeed. Once that discipline is in the therapist's marrow, once it doesn't even have to be thought about, then there will be time to explore ways of relaxing it. It's very hard to subject oneself to discipline after indulging in freedom. That's why students of art and

music are urged to master the discipline of their craft
before they attempt to transcend it.

Discarding the Therapist Mask

When all is said and done, nothing in our work may be
more important than our willingness to bring as much of
ourselves as possible to the therapeutic session. Whether a
given feeling or attitude is expressed in words is less
important than that we are *present* in the deepest and
fullest sense of that word. Understanding this imperative
does not resolve the dilemmas of what we should give our
clients, but it makes them less intimidating.

I work with students who are having their first experiences as therapists. One of the great satisfactions of this
work (both for them and for me) comes at the moment
students realize that when they enter the consulting room,
they don't need to don a therapist mask, a therapist voice,
a therapist posture, and a therapist vocabulary. They can
discard those accouterments because they have much,
much more than that to give their clients.

8

The New Relationship

~

I began this book by noting that for a long time the field of psychotherapy was sharply divided. Therapists who received their training from the psychoanalysts were taught the mysteries of transference along with a somewhat distant attitude toward their clients; those who were trained by the Rogerians and their humanistic descendants were encouraged to allow all their natural warmth and compassion into the consulting room but knew little or nothing of the values of working with the transference.

As I suggested in Chapter 1, some of the old conflicts are beginning to resolve themselves, a new harmony, a new consensus, has begun to emerge in respect to the clinical relationship. Granted, the harmony is not total, and major disagreements will undoubtedly remain. Still it is an exciting time, one in which ways are being found to integrate the insights of such therapists as Rogers and Kohut, whose concerns are for the human aspect of the client's experience, with those of therapists who, like Freud and Gill, maintain a steadfast belief in the power of the unconscious and the therapeutic leverage provided by the transference. In fact, Gill and Kohut themselves have gone a long way toward providing such integration.

Taken together, the views we have been considering suggest a way of conducting the clinical relationship. As I have noted, all therapists must develop their own way of working, a way that fits their personality and that honors their accumulating experience. But every therapist needs to start somewhere, and the findings and proposals described in this book provide a good starting place.

An Integration

Let's imagine ourselves therapists who have succeeded in integrating Freud, Rogers, Gill, and Kohut.

We will aspire to *genuineness:* we will strive to be transparent, not wearing our therapist mask and not pretending to be someone we're not.

And we will remember how important it is to find ways of letting our clients know that we consider them worthwhile persons.

We will be nondefensive. We have much to learn from the way our clients see us, particularly if it differs from the way we see ourselves. Gone forever is the old psychoanalytic fantasy that all the client's responses come only from ancient templates. Many of them are perfectly reasonable responses to what the therapist has done or who the therapist is. We must always be willing to ask ourselves what we have done to provoke any particular response, and we must always be willing to encourage the client to talk about it.

We will remind ourselves that when clients give us a bad time, they may be showing us the kind of bad time someone gave them long ago, and we will do well to stay open to that information.

It is essential that, whatever feelings clients express about us, our response will be interested, encouraging, and without judgment. It is likely that clients have previously gotten very different responses from significant people, and this difference is an important ingredient of the therapy. So whatever the stimulus, we do not preen when we are praised and do not punish when we are attacked. And we keep in mind that one of the most costly manifestations of defensiveness is self-justification.

We will allow ourselves a good deal of spontaneity. We will recognize that since we can't possibly be a blank screen, there is no reason to deny our clients our warmth and spontaneity.

We will view our clients with the utmost respect. When we think we know better than they what they should be doing in therapy, we will seriously consider the possibility that it is they who know better, and we will work hard at trying to discover the ways in which they are right. It has been humbling for me to learn from Kohut how readily I jump to the conclusion that my client is resisting or defending or acting out. And Kohut also reminded us how important it is to let clients *know* that we see what they're doing in a positive light.

Probably most important of all is the concept of empathy. We learn the most about clients by allowing ourselves to feel what they are feeling, to enter their world as if it were our own. We will remember Kohut's advice to do our best to see the world from the clients' point of view and let them know that that is what we are doing: we are seeing why what they are doing or what they are feeling makes sense from their perspective. Kohut teaches that it is hard to change and grow until someone has really *seen* where we are now. Our empathy is our major therapeutic contribution to our clients.

Thus our job is not to give advice, opinions, or answers, but continually to do our best to *understand* the client:

To understand what clients are experiencing and what they are *feeling* at this moment.

To understand the gradually unfolding coherence of the themes of their lives.

We will let our clients know that we *are* doing our best to understand them. When we don't understand, we'll ask for their help, and when we do think we understand something, we'll tell them so.

It is important to recognize that empathy is not a technique but an attitude. Beginning therapists are often taught the technique of *reflection*—that is, saying back to clients what they have just said. The hope is, of course, that reflection will convey empathy to the client. ("See, I *am* listening, and I did hear what you said.") That's certainly understandable. A therapist needs to say *something*, and reflection is a reasonably safe mode to fall back on when all else fails. There are undoubtedly times when reflection is an excellent way of letting clients know they have been understood and encouraging them to go on. But teaching a technique is probably not the best way to make a therapist empathic.

What therapists need to learn is less a technique or a group of techniques than ways of opening themselves, first to their clients' experiences and then to their own spontaneity. That spontaneity will reveal their own special, idiosyncratic way of communicating empathy at that moment.[1]

So we will let our clients know we have *understood*, and then we will find ways to let them know that their feelings are more than just understandable: we will let them know that, given their individual histories, we consider those feelings inevitable.

Increasing the Client's Awareness of the Relationship

As therapists who integrate the ideas of Freud, Rogers, Gill, and Kohut, we will give our clients a good deal of encouragement to reveal their feelings about us. The transference is where the action is. According to Gill's formula, therapeutic movement results when clients

1. *Re-experience* the ancient thoughts, feelings, and impulses that were originally connected to the situations that bred their current troubles.

2. Experience those thoughts, feelings, and impulses *in the presence of the person toward whom they are now directed.*

3. *Express* them to that person.

4. Have that expression met with interest, objectivity, and *acceptance.*

In normal intercourse it is often considered bad form to reveal one's feelings about one's companion. Clients have to learn that it is very good form here. We must encourage them to talk about their thoughts, feelings, and fantasies about us, as well as their fantasies about our thoughts, feelings, and fantasies. So we will be alert for those opportunities:

If a client says he's afraid that other people will reject him if he reveals his true feelings, we will give him plenty of room to explore this fear in his own terms and then wonder (aloud) if he has that fear about us.

If he complains about being surrounded by insensitive people, we will gently wonder if we could be among them.

If she talks about resenting her boss, after hearing everything she has to say about her boss, we will wonder if this could possibly be a disguised way of talking about us, and, if we see a way to do so, we will explore that possibility.

And since unremitting respect for the client is one of our guidelines, we will gracefully take no for an answer. And when the client does talk about us or acknowledges that the feelings she expresses about her boss may indeed also refer to us, we will accept those statements with empathic interest and without judgment.

When I first read Gill and set out to encourage my clients to talk more about our relationship, I'm afraid I got carried away. I rather seized them by the lapels at every opportunity and even sometimes when there wasn't an opportunity. If a client spoke of being angry at a lover or afraid of a co-worker or dependent on a parent, the words were hardly out of the client's mouth before I was bringing the conversation back to the client and me. It took me a while to discover that this wasn't such a good idea. In the first place, sometimes clients really need time to talk about those outside relationships, and in the second place, my less-than-sensitive precipitousness often failed. After a while I lost some of my new-convert eagerness and settled down to try to work with a little more restraint and a lot more patience.

I recognized, of course, that clients were concerned with matters other than their relationship with me, and that good therapy would certainly give them an opportunity to work extensively on those other matters. Nonetheless, I continued to believe (as I still believe) that our relationship was the richest therapeutic topic, and that the more time clients spent talking about that relationship, the better off we would be. So I saw myself faced with a new technical problem: How was I to make it safe for them to reveal their feelings about me? Or how might I encourage my client to go from the lover or boss or parent to me? I began to think of the topic of our relationship as a large, strong fish for which I was angling with a very light line. If I reeled it in too soon or too sharply, I would break the line and lose the fish. If I didn't reel it in at all, I'd never land it. So I learned to give it line and bring it in a little at a time, feeling carefully for what the line would take. I learned to give plenty of attention to *each client's* topic. In the first place, the topic is important to the client. And in the second place, I am fishing with a very light line. Sometimes after I have given a client plenty of line and I feel the line will take it, I reel in my fish pretty vigorously.

Therapist:	*(after a rather full discussion of the client's anxieties about his continuing dependency on his mother)* You know, it occurs to me that it wouldn't be surprising if you had some of those feelings about me.
Client:	No, I don't think so. I feel good about our relationship.
	(The therapist's thoughts run something like this: I do believe in taking no for an answer,

*and I am reluctant to impose my interpre-
tation on him. All the same, some of our
recent discussions do make it reasonable to
believe that I may be right about this one.
Soon I'll take no for an answer. But not
quite yet.)*

Therapist: Yes, I hear that. But it would be surprising if other feelings about me and about
our relationship didn't crop up from time
to time. And I think it's always helpful if
those feelings can be talked about. I'd like
to explore this a little further, if I may.

Client: OK.

Therapist: When we started working together, you
had some conflict about the very idea of
therapy. You thought it was somehow
shameful not to take care of your own
problems.

Client: I remember that.

Therapist: Lately you've been seeing the value in it
and saying that it's become important to
you. It would be understandable if those
feelings were to stir up some anxiety about
getting too dependent on me. Would it be
possible for us to explore that?

If that approach didn't get some kind of affirmative
response, I would then let it go and assume that either I
was wrong or it wasn't yet time for this concern to surface.
And, of course, another unsettling possibility is that I just
wasn't a good enough fisherman.

Attending to the Selfobject Transferences

Following Kohut, we will try to understand how clients see us and what they want from us. This effort will help us identify a *mirror*, *idealizing*, or *twinship* transference, and will alert us to the deficits in the development of the client's self. We will attempt not to fill the need but rather to acknowledge the importance of it and the pain caused by its lack of fulfillment.

Helping the Client Learn About the Power of the Past

Re-experiencing therapists don't believe that *by itself* rational understanding will effect much change in the client, and they know better than to get caught in the puzzle-solving game of figuring out and teaching clients how they got to where they are. Nonetheless, they believe it is necessary for clients to understand how their early experiences influence their present lives.

Re-experiencing therapists believe that the transference is the royal road to that understanding. For clients, learning how early experiences affect their relationship with the therapist is a powerful way to grasp just how influential those experiences still are.

Helping the client learn about the power of the past is usually not the first order of business. With most clients the therapist will spend much of the earlier phases of the therapy just trying to understand their experience and letting them know it has been understood. And the therapist will continually work to increase each client's awareness of the relationship with the therapist. Then, after a time, having begun to gain some understanding of a client and of the themes of that client's life, the therapist will begin to help the client see that reactions to the therapist are inevitably determined *in part* by the attitudes and expectations the client carries everywhere.

Becoming increasingly aware of the themes of the client's life, the therapist will be in a better and better position to help the client see that there is nothing bad about carrying those attitudes and expectations everywhere. Given the events of the client's life, they are fully understandable—in fact, highly likely.

Therapy as an Intersubjective Situation

Three aspects of the intersubjective view are helpful to remember:

1. We are not objective viewers and not the arbiters of reality. A little humility is appropriate.

2. It is not meaningful to assert that some of a client's responses to the therapist are reality based and some reflect transference. They are all reality based, for they begin with the actual stimulus complex that is the therapist. And they all reflect transference, for all perceptions are filtered through the organizing principles.

3. Once we have grasped points 1 and 2, we see our clients' responses to us as rich opportunities to help them examine and reflect upon their organizing principles.

The Question of Diagnosis

You will have noticed that I have not raised the question of diagnosis. It seems to me that the question of diagnosis divides therapists into two schools. Some therapists, when they begin work with a new client, devote a good deal of attention to making a diagnosis. They then set about shaping a style of therapy, including a way of relating, that fits the particular client. The way these therapists work with a client they have diagnosed as borderline, for instance, is very different from the way they work with a client they consider neurotic.[2] Other therapists think very little about diagnosis. They do their kind of therapy with every client who comes along. Many of these therapists decline to treat clients who have psychoses, who are severely retarded, or who have serious organic problems; but otherwise, they don't concern themselves much with separating clients into categories. They do, however, make a continual, moment-to-moment, automatic diagnosis. The way *this* client is at *this* moment determines how such a therapist relates to that client, and a sensitive therapist relates differently to different clients and to the same client at different times.

The therapists we are considering, Freud, Rogers, Gill, and Kohut, belong to this second group. Rogers, you will recall, is explicit about his view that diagnosis is of no use to a therapist. Freud and Gill believe that psychoanalysis is the treatment of choice for anybody capable of forming a genuine relationship with the therapist. Kohut began his study of self psychology with the belief that his therapy depended on an accurate differential diagnosis, but by the end of his life he had changed his mind; he had come to believe that all people with emotional problems suffer from deficits of the self and could benefit from his empathic therapy.

Consequently, the approach I have proposed does not depend on diagnosis (although this style of therapy would be difficult to do with a client in an extreme psychotic condition or with one who had a serious organic problem). Like all therapy, it assumes an attentive sensitivity to each client at each moment and further assumes that therapists' empathy will carefully tune their responses from moment to moment.

And When the Therapy Must Be Brief?

In Chapter 1 I noted that the economics of the future may dictate an increase in brief therapy and a corresponding decline in long-term therapy. We may well be consulted by clients who can see us for only five or ten sessions. However modest our goals will be with such clients, there is no reason why we cannot apply to our work with them the same principles that guide our work with longer-term clients.

Whatever the length of the therapy, it is important that the therapist:

Be genuine, respectful, and affirming of the client's reality.

Sets out to understand the client and make the client aware of that intent.

Attempts to help the client bring to the surface the buried principles that govern his or her life.

Communicates, above all, empathy to the client.

Since transference is a ubiquitous phenomenon, it may emerge and become available for exploration even in these few sessions. If it does, the therapist should welcome it with interest and encouragement.

And in these few sessions the therapist may get a glimpse of the deficits in the client's self and find a chance to give what may be the first empathic response the client has ever received to that deficit and the needs it has engendered.

As I said before, it won't be the same as years of therapy, but it will be a lot better than nothing.

In the Consulting Room

All of the therapists whose work we have been pondering have proposed well-articulated theories of personality, theories of psychopathology, and theories of psychotherapy. Yet as we read their works, we get an inescapable impression that when they are actually with the client, something else is as important to them as their theory. That something else is the quality of their presence. When they are at their best, they seem to bring to their clients an air of expectant curiosity, a readiness to be surprised, a willingness from moment to moment to have their minds changed. Perhaps empathy, when all is said and done, is putting one's own world aside and fully entering that of the client.

Our authors share another characteristic: they are remarkably courageous. A consulting room offers a lot of places to hide; therapists can get through years of work without ever having to learn how a client feels about them or about what they have just said. The therapists we have been studying do their best never to avoid that learning. Indeed, Gill and Kohut court it, believing that nothing more important can happen in that room.

At the moment of the existential encounter between therapist and client, the client's whole world is present. All of the client's significant past relationships, all of that person's most basic hopes and fears are there and are focused on the therapist. If we can make it possible for our clients to become aware that their worlds are coming to rest in us, and if we can be there, fully there, to receive their awareness and respond to it, the relationship cannot help but become therapeutic.

Suggested Readings

On Freud

The best introduction, or reintroduction, to Freud is *Five Lectures on Psychoanalysis*. It can be found in a paperback published by Norton or in *The Standard Edition of the Complete Psychological Works of Sigmund Freud*, published by the Hogarth Press and found in practically every library in the English-speaking world. In the Standard Edition, "Five Lectures" will be found in Volume 11, page 3.

Freud's two classic papers on transference are short, and very interesting. They can be found in a paperback collection of Freud's papers called *Therapy and Technique*, edited by Philip Rieff, published by Macmillan's Collier Division. These papers can also be found in Volume 12 of the *Standard Edition*, the first, "The Dynamics of Transference," starting on page 99; the second, "Observations on Transference Love," starting on page 149.

On Rogers

Probably the best single introduction to Carl Rogers is his *On Becoming a Person* (Houghton Mifflin, 1961). I also highly recommend a short paper by Rogers, "The Necessary and Sufficient Conditions of Therapeutic Personality Change," *Journal of Consulting Psychology*, 21(2), 1957, 95–103. It is said that Rogers considered it his best paper. It certainly is a good one.

An excellent and highly readable text on the Rogerian approach is *Person-Centered Counseling in Action*, by Dave Mearns and Brian Thorne (Sage, 1988). A somewhat less accessible, but very solid and scholarly Rogerian discussion of the clinical relationship, is C. H. Patterson's *The Therapeutic Relationship* (Brooks/Cole, 1985).

On Gill

Gill's definitive book on the client–therapist relationship is *The Analysis of Transference,* Volume I (International Universities Press, 1982). Volume 2 of that book, by Gill and Irwin Hoffman, is an extremely valuable series of verbatim transcripts of therapy sessions, annotated to illustrate what the authors consider good and bad instances of the handling of the clinical relationship.

On Kohut

I think the best single book of Kohut's is the posthumously published *How Does Analysis Cure?* (The University of Chicago Press, 1984). It gives a comprehensive picture of his view of therapy and is more easily read than his earlier books. His other two major works, *The Analysis of the Self* (1971) and *The Restoration of the Self* (1977), both published by International Universities Press, are not easy, but they are required reading for anyone wishing to delve deeply into Kohut's thought.

An excellent book that gives a clear and complete picture of Kohut's work is *Empathic Attunement: The "Technique" of Psychoanalytic Self-Psychology,* by Crayton Rowe and David MacIsaac (Jason Aronson, 1989).

Perhaps the most accessible of all is *The Theory and Practice of Self Psychology,* by Marjorie Taggart White and Marcella Bakur Weiner, published in New York by Brunner/Mazel (1986).

On Countertransference

Heinrich Racker's *Transference and Countertransference* (International Universities Press, 1968) is still the classic work on countertransference.

A very good contemporary book on the topic is *Understanding Countertransference,* by Michael Tansey and Walter Burke (Analytic Press, 1989).

Thomas Ogden's *Projective Identification and Psychotherapeutic Technique,* published by Jason Aronson (1982), is a fine introduction to the concept of projective identification.

On Existential Psychology

For a rich taste of an existential psychotherapist at work, Irvin Yalom's *Love's Executioner* (Basic Books, 1989) is highly recommended; for a more complete description of existential psychotherapy, you might look at Yalom's *Existential Psychotherapy* (Basic Books, 1980).

All of Rollo May's books are extremely useful for an understanding of the existential perspective. I particularly like *Love and Will* (W. W. Norton, 1969), *Psychology and the Human Dilemma* (D. Van Nostrand, 1967), and May's edited volume *Existential Psychology*, 2nd ed. (Random House, 1969).

On Intersubjectivity

Influenced by the work of both Gill and Kohut, *Psychoanalytic Treatment: An Intersubjective Approach* (Analytic Press, 1987), by R. D. Stolorow, B. Brandchaft, and G. E. Atwood, adds an innovative and extremely useful perspective.

The same authors have edited an excellent book on intersubjectivity: *The Intersubjective Perspective*, published by Jason Aronson (1994).

Darlene Bregman Ehrenberg's *Intimate Edge* is well worth exploring. It is published in New York by W. W. Norton (1992).

General

An intelligent and searching study of the clinical relationship from a contemporary psychoanalytic point of view is Roy Schafer's *Analytic Attitude* (Basic Books, 1982), which has become a classic in the field.

A fine little book that discusses our topic from a Jungian perspective is Mario Jacoby's *Analytic Encounter* (Inner City Books, 1984).

Notes

⤳

Preface

1. Salinger, J. D. (1959). *Raise high the roof beam, carpenters, and Seymour, an introduction* (p. 187). Boston: Little, Brown.

1. Why Study the Relationship?

1. Breuer, J., & Freud, S. (1895). Studies in hysteria. In J. Strachey (Ed. and Trans.), *The standard edition of the complete psychological works of Sigmund Freud* (Vol. 2, pp. ix–323). London: Hogarth.

2. Freud, S. (1905). Fragment of an analysis of a case of hysteria. In *The standard edition* (Vol. 7, pp. 7–122) (1909). Notes upon a case of obsessional neurosis. In *The standard edition* (Vol. 10, pp. 153–318).

3. Rogers, C. (1942). *Counseling and psychotherapy.* Boston: Houghton Mifflin.

4. Schutz, W. C. (1980). Encounter therapy. In R. J. Corsini (Ed.), *Current psychotherapies.* Itasca, IL: F. E. Peacock.

5. Sullivan, B. S. (1989). *Psychotherapy grounded in the feminine principle.* Wilmette, IL: Chiron.

6. Kohut, H. (1971). *The analysis of the self.* New York: International Universities Press; Gill, M. M. (1982). *The analysis of transference.* New York: International Universities Press.

7. May, R. (1960). The emergence of existential psychology. In R. May (Ed.), *Existential psychology* (p. 14). New York: Random House.

2. The Discovery of Transference: Sigmund Freud

1. Chodorow, N. (1978). *The reproduction of mothering.* Berkeley: University of California Press (1989). *Feminism and psychoanalytic theory.* New Haven: Yale University Press.

2. Freud, S. (1912). The dynamics of transference. In J. Strachey (Ed. and Trans.), *The standard edition of the complete psychological works of Sigmund Freud* (Vol. 12, pp. 97–108). London: Hogarth.

3. Freud, S. (1920). Beyond the pleasure principle. In *The standard edition* (Vol. 18, p. 22).

4. Freud. The dynamics of transference, pp. 97–108.

5. Freud, S. (1915). Observations on transference love. In *The standard edition* (Vol. 12, pp. 157–171).

6. Freud, S. (1905). Fragment of an analysis of a case of hysteria. In *The standard edition* (Vol. 7, pp. 7–122).

7. Freud, S. (1917). Introductory lectures on psychoanalysis, Lecture XXVIII. In *The standard edition* (Vol. 16, p. 436).

8. Freud, S. (1914). Remembering, repeating, and working through. In *The standard edition* (Vol. 12, pp. 145–156).

9. Freud. Introductory lectures, Lecture XXVIII, p. 454.

10. Freud, S. (1940). An outline of psychoanalysis. In *The standard edition* (Vol. 23, p. 177); italics added.

11. Freud, S. (1937). Analysis terminable and interminable. In *The standard edition* (Vol. 23, pp. 211–253).

3. The Influence of the Humanists: Carl Rogers

1. Rogers, C. (1942). *Counseling and psychotherapy.* Boston: Houghton Mifflin.

2. Rogers, C. R., & Dymond, R. F. (Eds.). (1954). *Psychotherapy and personality change.* Chicago: University of Chicago Press.

3. Rogers, C. R. (1957). The necessary and sufficient conditions of therapeutic personality change. *Journal of Consulting Psychology, 21,* 95–103.

4. Rogers, C. R. (1962). The interpersonal relationship: The core of guidance. In C. R. Rogers & B. Stevens (Eds.), *Person to person* (pp. 91–92). Lafayette, CA: Real People Press.

5. Ibid., p. 93.

6. Truax, C. B., & Carkhuff, R. R. (1967). *Toward effective counseling and psychotherapy: Training and practice.* Chicago: Aldine.

7. Rogers. The necessary and sufficient conditions.

8. Rogers, C. R. (1970). *Carl Rogers on encounter groups.* New York: Harper & Row.

9. Rogers. The necessary and sufficient conditions.

10. Rogers, C. R. (1961). *On becoming a person* (pp. 163–182). Boston: Houghton Mifflin.

11. Rogers. The interpersonal relationship, p. 97.

12. Rogers. *On becoming a person,* pp. 184–185.

4. A Re-experiencing Therapy: Merton Gill

1. Gill, M. M. (1982). *The analysis of transference* (Vol. 1). New York: International Universities Press.

2. Gill, M. M. (1982). The point of view of psychoanalysis: Energy discharge or person? *Psychoanalysis and Contemporary Thought, 4,* 523–551.

3. Freud, S. (1915). Repression. In J. Strachey (Ed. & Trans.), *The standard edition of the complete psychological works of Sigmund Freud* (Vol. 14, pp. 143–158). London: Hogarth (1926). Inhibitions, symptoms, and anxiety, ibid. (Vol. 20, pp. 77–175) (1940). An outline of psychoanalysis, ibid. (Vol. 23, pp. 139–207).

4. Freud, S. (1914). Remembering, repeating, and working through. In *The standard edition* (Vol. 12, pp. 145–156).

5. Freud, S. (1917). Introductory lectures on psychoanalysis, Lecture XXVII. In *The standard edition* (Vol. 16, p. 444).

6. Gill. *The analysis of transference,* p. 44.

7. Beck, A. T. (1976). *Cognitive therapy and the emotional disorders.* New York: International Universities Press.

8. Gill. *The analysis of transference,* pp. 15–27.

9. Ibid., pp. 64–66.

10. Ibid., pp. 20–21.

11. Ibid., p. 109.

12. Ibid., pp. 86–88.

13. Gill. *The point of view of psychoanalysis,* p. 543.

14. Gill, M. M. (1994). *Psychoanalysis in transition* (pp. 1–13). Hillsdale, NJ: Analytic Press.

15. Stolorow, R. D. (1994). The intersubjective context of intrapsychic experience. In R. Stolorow, G. E. Atwood, & B. Brandchaft (Eds.), *The intersubjective perspective.* (pp. 3–14). Northvale, NJ: Jason Aronson; Hoffman, I. Z. (1991). Discussion: Toward a social-constructivist view of the analytic situation. *Psychoanalytic Dialogues, 1,* 74–105.

16. Hoffman, I. Z. (1992). Some practical implications of the social-constructivist view of the psychoanalytic situation. *Psychoanalytic Dialogues, 2,* 287–304; Stolorow, R. (1994). The nature and therapeutic action of psychoanalytic interpretation. In Stolorow et al., *The intersubjective perspective,* pp. 43–55.

17. Gill, M. M. (1984). Transference: A change in conception or only in emphasis? A response. *Psychoanalytic Inquiry, 4,* 499.

18. Gill. *The point of view of psychoanalysis,* p. 544.

19. Gill. *The analysis of transference,* pp. 107–127.

20. Ibid., pp. 107–114.

21. Gill. *The point of view of psychoanalysis,* pp. 545–546.

5. The Meeting of Psychoanalysis and Humanism: Heinz Kohut

1. Kohut, H. (1977). *The restoration of the self* (p. 227). New York: International Universities Press.

2. Gill, M. M. (1994). Heinz Kohut's self psychology. In *A decade of progress: Progress in self psychology* (Vol. 10, pp. 197–211). Hillsdale, NJ: Analytic Press.

3. Kohut, H. (1968). The psychoanalytic treatment of narcissistic personality disorders. In P. H. Ornstein (Ed.), *The search for the self* (Vol. 1, pp. 506–507). New York: International Universities Press.

4. Kohut, H. (1971). *The analysis of the self.* New York: International Universities Press.

5. Kohut, H. (1984). *How does analysis cure?* (pp. 192–193). Chicago: University of Chicago Press.

6. Kohut. *The analysis of the self,* pp. 123–124.

7. Ibid., pp. 49–50.

8. Kohut, H., & Wolf, E. S. (1978). The disorders of the self and their treatment: An outline. *International Journal of Psychoanalysis, 59,* 413–425.

9. Kohut. *The analysis of the self,* pp. 7–11.

10. Kohut. *How does analysis cure?* pp. 198–200.

11. Ibid., p. 99.

12. Ibid., p. 70.

13. Kohut. *The restoration of the self,* pp. 180–184.

14. Greenberg, J. R., & Mitchell, S. A. (1983). *Object relations in psychoanalytic theory.* Cambridge, MA: Harvard University Press.

15. Alexander, F., & French, T. (1946). *Psychoanalytic psychotherapy.* New York: Ronald Press.

16. Kohut. *How does analysis cure?* p. 78.

17. Ibid., p. 82.

18. Goldberg, A. (Ed.). (1978). *The psychology of the self* (pp. 447–448). New York: International Universities Press.
19. Kohut. *How does analysis cure?* pp. 76–77.
20. Kohut. *The restoration of self*, pp. 84–88.
21. Kohut. *How does analysis cure?* pp. 93–94.
22. Ibid., pp. 70–71.
23. Ibid., pp. 192–210.
24. Stolorow, R., Brandchaft, B., & Atwood, G. (1987). *Psychoanalytic treatment.* (pp. 101–103). Hillsdale, NJ: Analytic Press.
25. Kohut & Wolf. *Disorders of the self*, p. 421.
26. Ibid., p. 421.
27. Kohut. *How does analysis cure?* pp. 193–210.
28. Ibid., p. 221.

6. Countertransference

1. Freud, S. (1910). The future prospects of psychoanalytic therapy. In J. Strachey (Ed. & Trans.), *The standard edition of the complete psychological works of Sigmund Freud* (Vol. 11, pp. 141–151). London: Hogarth.
2. Heimann, P. (1950). On countertransference. *International Journal of Psychoanalysis, 31,* 81–84.
3. Racker, H. (1968). *Transference and countertransference.* New York: International Universities Press.
4. Tansey, M. J., & Burke, W. F. (1989). *Understanding countertransference.* Hillsdale, NJ: Analytic Press.
5. Klein, M. (1946). Notes on some schizoid mechanisms. *International Journal of Psychoanalysis, 33,* 433–438.
6. Grinberg, L. (1979). Projective counteridentification and countertransference. In L. Epstein and A. H. Feiner (Eds.), *Countertransference.* New York: Jason Aronson.
7. Ogden, T. H. (1982). *Projective identification and psychotherapeutic technique* (p. 4). Northvale, NJ: Jason Aronson.

7. The Therapist's Dilemmas

1. Rangell, L. (1969). The psychoanalytic process. *International Journal of Psychoanalysis, 49,* 19–26.

2. Schutz, W. C. (1980). Encounter therapy. In R. J. Corsini (Ed.), *Current psychotherapies.* Itasca, IL: F. E. Peacock.

3. May, R. (1958). Contributions of existential psychotherapy. In R. May, E. Angel, & H. F. Ellenberger (Eds.), *Existence.* New York: Basic Books.

4. Rogers, C. R. (1962). The interpersonal relationship: The core of guidance. In C. R. Rogers & B. Stevens (Eds.), *Person to person* (pp. 91–92). Lafayette, CA: Real People Press.

5. Stolorow, R. D., Brandchaft, B., & Atwood, G. E. (1987). *Psychoanalytic treatment: An intersubjective approach.* Hillsdale, NJ: Analytic Press.

6. Stolorow, R., Atwood, G. E., & Brandchaft, B. (Eds.). (1994). *The intersubjective perspective.* (pp. 3–14). Northvale, NJ: Jason Aronson.

7. Ehrenberg, D. B. (1992). *The intimate edge.* New York: W. W. Norton; Mitchell, S. A. (1991). Wishes, needs, and interpersonal negotiations. *Psychoanalytic Inquiry, 11,* 147–170.

8. Maroda, K. J. (1991). *The power of countertransference.* Northvale, NJ: Jason Aronson.

8. The New Relationship

1. Bozarth, J. (1984). Beyond reflection: emergent modes of empathy. In R. F. Levant & J. M. Shlein (Eds.), *Client-centered therapy and the person-centered approach.* New York: Praeger.

2. Masterson, J. F. (1976). *Psychotherapy of the borderline adult.* New York: Brunner/Mazel.

Index